Medieval West Africa

VIEWS FROM ARAB SCHOLARS
AND MERCHANTS

Medieval West Africa

Views from Arab Scholars and Merchants

Edited by

NEHEMIA LEVTZION

and

JAY SPAULDING

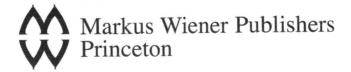

Markus Wiener Publishers
Princeton

Third printing, 2011
Copyright © 2003 by Nehemia Levtzion and Jay Spaulding

Excerpts from *Corpus of Early Arabic Sources for West African History*,
edited by Nehemia Levtzion and J.F.P. Hopkins, were reprinted
by permission of Cambridge University Press.

For information write to:
Markus Wiener Publishers
231 Nassau Street, Princeton, NJ 08542
www.markuswiener.com

Library of Congress Cataloging-in-Publication Data
Levtzion, Nehemia.
    Medieval West Africa : views from Arab Scholars and Merchants
    Nehemia Levtzion, Jay Spaulding.
        Includes bibliographical references and index.
        ISBN-13: 978-1-55876-304-3 (hc)
        ISBN-10: 1-55876-304-X (hc)
        ISBN-13: 978-1-55876-305-0 (pbk.)
        ISBN-10: 1-55876-305-8 (pbk.)
    1. Africa, West—History—To 1884—Sources.
    2. Africa, West—History—To 1884.
    I. Spaulding, Jay. II. Title.
    DT476 .L49 2002
    966'.021--dc21
    2002151333

Contents

Preface

This book, designed for students, offers an English translation of meaningful selections from Arabic works about West Africa before 1500 by major writers of the Islamic heartlands.

Scholars doing research and students of Arabic should consult the comprehensive collection of these sources: N. Levtzion and J.F.P. Hopkins, eds., *Corpus of Early Arabic Sources for West African History* (Princeton, N.J.: Markus Wiener, 2006).

Because this book is intended for students who do not study Arabic, bars and dots for the transliteration of Arabic words have been left out. Spelling and punctuation have been Americanized, and a few minor corrections made to the translations. Also, the full references to the published editions of the Arabic texts may be consulted only in the comprehensive *Corpus*.

Each of the twenty-two texts is preceded by a short introduction, with some biographical details, the author's sources concerning *bilad al-sudan*, and indications of what new information the text added to what had already been known.

Preface

Introduction

The View from Behind the Curtain

Kingdoms arose during the early centuries of the Common Era across a wide zone of West Africa that lay south of the Sahara Desert and north of the forest belt that adjoined the Atlantic Ocean. Archaeology has begun to provide sound information about early chapters of this story, while oral traditions preserved among living West African communities have contributed their own vision of this remote past. Another rich source of information about West Africa is available in the Arabic sources written by geographers and chroniclers in the Muslim world between the eighth and the fifteenth centuries.

During those eight centuries the Arabic language helped unify the culturally diverse realm of Islam by serving as a universal medium for administration, commerce, and scholarship. With the passage of time both the faith of Islam itself and many other aspects of Islamic civilization pressed on beyond the boundaries determined by conquest to influence neighboring communities, thus creating a still wider cultural universe. West Africa north of the forest became partially incorporated into this wider universe of medieval Islam. The region acquired a name in Arabic that was destined to endure; it was, and remains, *bilad al-sudan*, the land of black people.

The purpose of the present general introduction is to show where and how the Arabic sources dealt with some major themes related to the history of *bilad al-sudan*. This discussion is by no means comprehensive, and the reader is invited to further explore the sources and use them as building stones in attempting to arrive at the reconstruction of the past.

These writings carry very great value as sources for the history of West Africa; however, they also have some peculiarities and limitations. All the sources offered here were written by outsiders, by Muslims who lived north of the Sahara. Only one of those writers, Ibn Battuta, visited the land of the Sudan himself. Others recorded accounts from informants who had visited the place.

The transmission of knowledge across cultural boundaries is never easy, as one comparatively minor but nevertheless conspicuous example may illustrate. The sound systems of West African languages differ significantly from that of Arabic, so that attempts to convey African names or terms in Arabic characters sometimes produced strange results. One author (Ibn Battuta) took pains to spell out a number of African words as accurately as possible by scrupulously adding the short vowels that are ordinarily omitted in Arabic as unnecessary. Most authors, however, rendered African words strictly in terms of consonants and long vowels. In preparing this book the editors have whenever possible translated the strange spellings of the medieval texts into more familiar modern form. In some cases, however, and particularly when no modern version of the word is known, the actual Arabic rendition is given; for example, the capital of the empire of Mali must remain BYTY. It is sobering to consider how much that is unknown may lie concealed behind the words we have transliterated because we cannot translate them. The problem of rendering African words in Arabic letters, moreover, is merely one tiny example of a much broader range of cultural barriers that separated the medieval authors in Arabic from the West African people they undertook to describe.

An interesting theme to unfold gradually over time among the sources considered below is the attempt by the Arabic writers of the

Middle Ages to locate Sudanese places spatially in relation to long-familiar sites of the Mediterranean world and the Middle East. One approach, derived from the Greeks and ancestral to the modern notions of latitude and longitude, drew imaginary lines from east to west that divided the (known) world into a series of parallel "climes," each of which could then be divided by north-south divisions into a row of segments, usually ten, arranged from west to east. An attempt was then made to fit each newly identified place in West Africa into its appropriate clime and segment. A second method for the organization of geographical information drew upon Iranian tradition and divided the (known) world into seven parts, of which North and West Africa comprised one. Two of the writers had their own individual systems, one of which (al-Zuhri's) also divided the world into seven parts, but different parts, while the other (Ibn Hawqal's) made twenty divisions.

A related problem, a reflection of the influence of Ptolemy's "Geography," most emphatically developed by al-Idrisi (p. 36), was the false concept that the lands of the Sudan were dry and scorching without any rain. He therefore described the route from Mali to Ghana as crossing "over dunes and deep sands" (p. 32). As a result, he considered it vital that all Sudanic settlements must of necessity be located along a river, but also that all the rivers of Africa were one, the Nile. This "Nile" of the medieval imagination therefore meanders through the pages to follow on a wildly improbable course past virtually every named African settlement from Senegal to Nubia and Egypt.

These acknowledged limitations, once noticed and taken into consideration, do not diminish the value of the Arabic sources for the numerous themes to which they do offer testimony. The following sections of this introductory essay will highlight some of these themes, with some references to the texts in this collection.

Some Notes on Customs and Manners

Medieval Arabic authors typically conveyed and interpreted history in terms of genealogies. The fact that all humans were descended from a single forefather implied that the communities of *bilad al-sudan* were distant kinsmen whose correct place on the family tree of humanity could be determined. They tell the story of the migration to West Africa from the Middle East of the children of Ham, son of Noah (see al-Yaʿqubi p. 1).

Over the course of the centuries Islam became increasingly important in West Africa, and the alien authors tended to exaggerate the importance of West African leaders and groups perceived to be praiseworthy because of their friendship and respect to Muslims, even though they themselves remained pagans (see al-Bakri pp. 14, 15).

In the present section we shall refer to some customs and manners of the people of the Western Sudan as described in the Arabic sources. These references appear more prominently in the earlier centuries before the progress of Islam.

Al-Bakri has the most interesting ethnographic data about customs and manners. The people of Zafqu (probably those later spelled as Zafun) were "a nation of Sudan who worship a certain snake." This snake even picked the chosen king (p. 14). In Ghana, al-Bakri (p. 15) described the groves and thickets that surrounded the king's town, where their sorcerers lived and their idols and the kings' tombs were found. "These woods are guarded and none may enter them and know what is there. In them also are the king's prisons. If somebody is imprisoned there no news of him is ever heard again." In these thickets the king is buried; "when their king dies they construct over the place where his tomb will be an enormous dome of acacia wood. ... At his side they place his ornaments, his weapons, and the vessels from which he used to eat and drink, filled with various kinds of food and beverages. They place there too the men who used to serve his meals." According to al-Bakri (p. 20) "the custom of trial by water exists in the land of Ghana." The accused is made to drink bitter water, and if he vomits his innocence is recognized.

Al-ʿUmari (p. 55) recorded from his Egyptian informants, who had met Mansa Musa and his people, "that in the territory of the infidels adjacent to their country the elephant is hunted by magic." Al-ʿUmari has more accounts of magic and sorcery: "In all the countries, especially Ghana, sorcery is much employed. They are forever litigating before their king because of it, saying: 'Such-a-one has killed my brother, or son, or daughter, or sister, by sorcery.' The killer is sentenced to punishment by retaliation and the sorcerer is put to death."

There are few references to alleged cannibalism of people who "eat anyone who falls into their hands" (al-Bakri p. 21; cf. Ibn Battuta p. 84).

We shall conclude this brief section with a stereotypic description of those peoples who had not yet been exposed to outside influences: "[they] are naked and do not cover themselves with anything at all. They marry without paying any dower or bride-price. Of all people they are the most prolific. . . . Peoples of the neighboring countries continually capture them, using various tricks. They take them away to their own lands, and sell them in droves to the merchants. Every year great numbers of them are sent to Morocco. Everyone in the land of Lamlam is branded on the face with fire, which is their mark . . ." (al-Idrisi p. 31)

Encounters with Islam: Cultural and Religious Change

The Arabic sources follow closely the progress of Islam. At the end of the ninth century, according to al-Yaʿqubi (p. 3), the king of Awdaghust had no religion or law. A century later, towards the end of the tenth century, al-Muhallabi (p. 7) described the people of Awdhaghust as Muslims. Al-Muhallabi, who lived at the court of the Fatimid caliphs in Cairo, attributed the conversion of the people of Awdaghust to the Isma'ili Mahdi 'Ubayd Allah (909–934). This is, however, unlikely because according to al-Bakri (p. 11) most of the inhabitants of Awdaghust were from Ibadi communities in Ifriqiya.

Islam in West Africa, as in North African Islam, is uniformly Maliki. The consolidation of Malikism was the work of the Almoravids in the eleventh century, who eradicated heretical groups in North Africa. In the Western Sudan the Almoravids put an end to the growing influence of the Ibadis, a sub-sect of the Khawarij.

Al-Muhallabi (p. 8) provided the first account of Islam in a Sudanic kingdom. The king of Kawkaw "pretends to be a Muslim and most of them pretend to be Muslims too." This statement is clarified by al-Bakri (pp. 21–22). The people of Kawkaw worship idols, but their king is a Muslim, "for they entrust the kingship only to Muslims." This Muslim king, however, is surrounded by pre-Islamic customs. When the king sits down to eat "nobody in the town goes about his business until he has finished his repast." Islam at the court of the eleventh century king of Gao may be considered typical of Islam in the courts of other West African kingdoms.

Islam expanded southwards with the extension of trade routes to the goldfields. Closer to the goldfields "no Muslims live there but when they enter their country the inhabitants treat them with respect and step out of their way." The outpost of Islam was the town of Yarisna, "inhabited by Muslims surrounded by polytheists" (al-Bakri p. 17).

The initial process of conversion is described by al-Bakri (pp. 18–19) for the small chiefdom of Malal. Its king converted after a Muslim resident had saved the country from severe drought: "So the king ordered the idols to be broken and expelled the sorcerers from his country. He and his descendants after him as well as his nobles were sincerely attached to Islam, while the common people of his kingdom remained polytheists." In Malal, as in Kawkaw, the king and his entourage became Muslims while the common people adhered to their own religion. Because a king could not cut himself off from his people, pre-Islamic customs persisted also at the court. One result, as reported by al-Bakri (p. 20), was that a certain king is said to be a Muslim, "but he conceals his religion."

At the same time in Takrur, on the lower Senegal and in close contact with the Almoravids of the southern Sahara, a new ruler Warjabi b. Rabis "embraced Islam, introduced among them Islamic religious law and compelled them to observe it." He also converted the neighbouring people of Silla. All this took place before 1040, the year Warjabi died (al-Bakri p. 13). This was an isolated case of Islamic militancy.

An earlier phase in the process of Islamization is described by al-Bakri (pp. 15–16) in Ghana, where the king is not a Muslim, but "his interpreters, the official in charge of his treasury and the majority of his ministers are Muslims." A non-Muslim king is praised "on account of his love of justice and friendship for the Muslims." The Muslims were exempted from local practices. They were not obliged to sprinkle dust on their heads, but greeted the king "by clapping their hands."

This was a transitional period, because Ghana converted less than ten years after al-Bakri's description, in 1076 according to al-Zuhri (p. 25). It is significant, however, that around 1200, the governor of Sijilmasa wrote to the king of Ghana, saying: "We are neighbors in benevolence, even if we differ in religion" (al-Sarakhsi p. 38). The setback for Islam in Ghana was probably the result of its conquest by the non-Muslim Susu from the south. See Ibn Khaldun (p. 92) for a traditional account of the conquest of Ghana by the Susu.

Ibn Sa'id (p. 44), writing in 1286, says that the king of Kanim who converted to Islam was the great-great-great-grandfather of the ruling king. Four generations back would take us to about 1100. By the fourteenth century, according to al-'Umari (p. 52), the people of Kanim were "rigid in religion." Indeed there is enough evidence to assert that Islam spread wider and deeper among the common people of Kanim and Borno than elsewhere in West Africa.

Most of the text of al-ʿUmari is dedicated to Mali. Mansa Musa, the famous pilgrim-king of Mali, "built ordinary and cathedral mosques and minarets, and established the Friday observances, and prayers in congregation, and the muezzin's call. He brought jurists of the Malikite School to his country and there continued as sultan of the Muslims and became a student of religious sciences." (al-ʿUmari p. 53)

Al-ʿUmari gathered information on Mali in Egypt. Ibn Battuta, on the other hand, provided eyewitness information about the state of Islam in Mali. His host in the capital of Mali, Muhammad Ibn al-Faqih, was married to a cousin of the sultan of Mali (Ibn Battuta p. 71). Ibn al-Faqih, together with the *qadi* and the *khatib,* were frequent visitors to the king's palace, where on occasions they recited the Koran to the king (p. 72). The *khatib* and the Muslim scholars were formally seated in the audience of the king (p. 73). The mosque and the house of the *khatib* were sanctuaries (p. 80).

The medieval authors alluded to the five pillars of Islam that every Muslim must observe. The first of these, evident in stories of conversion, was the profession of faith, the *shahada* in Arabic. This is indeed what the Muslim asked the king of Malal in the account of al-Bakri (p. 18): "O King, if you believed in God (who is exalted) and testified that He is One, and testified as to the prophetic mission of Muhammad (may God bless him and grant him peace)." The second pillar is the prayer. Ibn Battuta (p. 82) praises the Muslims of Mali for "their assiduity in prayer and their persistence in performing it in congregation . . . . If it is a Friday and a man does not go early to the mosque he will not find anywhere to pray because of the press of the people." The third pillar is the fast of Ramadan, which the king of Mali and his courtiers observed (Ibn Battuta p. 82). The fourth pillar is the obligation to give alms to the poor. Though we do not have a clear reference to giving alms, the political system, as we shall indicate later, is based on redistribution of the wealth accumulated by the king, which must have included also the giving of alms. The final obligation was the pilgrimage (*hajj*). Ibn Khaldun (pp. 90–91) mentions several kings of Mali who performed the pilgrimage to Mecca. Al-Qalqashandi (p. 104) and *al-Khabar*, attributed to al-Maqrizi (p. 108), recorded two kings of Kanim, a father and a son, al-Hajj Ibrahim and al-Hajj Idris, whose titles indicate that they performed the pilgrimage. Ibn Battuta (p. 76) mentioned al-Hajj Musa al-Wanjarati, who came as an ambassador from Mansa Sulayman of Mali to the Moroccan Sultan Abu'l-Hasan. Ibn Khaldun (p. 94) met in Cairo al-Hajj Yunus, *turjman* (translated as interpreter, but probably the ambassador) of Mali in Egypt.

The two major Muslim festivals, the Feast of Sacrifice on 10 Dhu'l-Hijja and the Feast of Fast-breaking on 1 Shawwal, became official events in the Islamized kingdoms. The people of Kanim see their veiled king only during the two festivals, when he is seen at dawn and in the afternoon (al-ʿUmari p. 51). Ibn Battuta was present at the court of Mali during the two major festivals. Whereas in the morning the king participated in the festival's public prayer, in the afternoon a traditional ceremony took place in which bards dressed as birds recounted the history of the kingdom (p. 78). Ibn Battuta considered this custom among the acts of which he disapproved, together with their custom of sprinkling of dust and ashes on their heads and the habit that women appear before men naked. He did approve of their diligence in prayer and "their eagerness to memorize the great Koran" (pp. 81–83).

The African Tradition of Statecraft

When the earliest report came from the pen of al-Yaʿqubi (p. 2) towards the end of the ninth century, there were three great kingdoms south of the Sahara: Kanim, Kawkaw (Gao), and Ghana. Kawkaw and Ghana had already developed into large-scale states: "there are a number of kingdoms whose rulers pay allegiance to him and acknowledge his sovereignty." This model of an "empire," a loose structure of minor kingdoms that make up the provinces, might be read also from later reports in the Arabic sources.

Most of the smaller kingdoms and all of the larger ones, in addition to their dominant ethnic core, also incorporated numerous peripheral groups of subjects, whose lesser kings served the emperor as subordinate lords. In eleventh-century Ghana the sons of the vassal lords resided at court, "wearing splendid garments and their hair plaited with gold," but also serving as political hostages for the good behavior of their distant fathers (al-Bakri, p. 16). Ibn Kathir (p. 114) was told, for example, that Mansa Musa of Mali had "24 kings under his authority, each having people and soldiers under him." As al-ʿUmari explained (p. 53), "The province of Mali is the one where the king's capital, BYTY, is situated. All these other provinces are subordinate to it and the same name Mali, which is the name of the chief province of this kingdom, is given to them collectively." Or, as al-Yaʿqubi (p. 2) learned concerning the high king of Kawkaw, "there are a number of kingdoms whose rulers pay allegiance to him and acknowledge his sovereignty, although they are kings in their own lands." The king of Kanim, according to al-Khabar (p. 108), "has five [lesser] kings under his sway." Beneath the subordinate kings in the structure of government stood the diverse leaders of the communities of subjects.

The name by which a kingdom of the western Sudan came to be known might derive from any of several sources, including the name of a dominant ethnic group, the title of a ruler, or the capital city. Ibn Khaldun (pp. 92–93) refers to the Ghana, Susu, and Mali as political units as well as ethnic groups. According to al-Muhallabi (p. 8), Kawkaw "is the name of a people and a country of the Sudan." In other cases the name by which a kingdom came to be known to outsiders might also be said to derive from the title of its ruler; according to al-Bakri (pp. 14, 18) the name of "Ghana," like the less familiar "Daw," was a royal title. Sometimes the

xx

name of the capital was extended to mean the whole realm; "then there is the kingdom of Kawkaw . . . . Kawkaw is the name of the town," explained al-Ya'qubi (p. 2). For Yakut (p. 40), the name of Zafun derived from that of its principal town, while for al-Bakri (p. 17), Gharantal was "a big town and a mighty kingdom."

Every subject could appeal directly to the king for justice. According to al-Idrisi (p. 34), a town called Tiraqqa was subject to the king of Ghana, "to whom people go in litigation." Al-Idrisi (pp. 32–33) also describes the morning parade in Ghana, "the king mounts his horse and rides at the head of his officers through the lanes of the town and around it. Anyone who has suffered injustice or misfortune confronts him, and stays there until the wrong is remedied." In fourteenth century Mali, according to al-'Umari (p. 57), "complaints and appeals against administrative oppression are placed before the king and he delivers judgment upon them himself."

Ibn Battuta (p. 69) praised the security of roads in Mali. He (p. 79) described how a Massuta merchant sought justice from Mansa Sulayman against the *mushrif*, the Sultan's commercial agent in Walata, who paid him 100 mithqals for something worth 600 mithqals. The king called his agent from Walata, and after the merchant's due was established "the *mushrif* was relieved of his office." On the other hand, when a certain white *qadi* made a false claim that he had been robbed, Mansa Musa banished him to the land of the infidels who eat mankind, where he stayed for four years (Ibn Battuta, p. 84). Ibn Battuta (pp. 81–82) was impressed by the lack of oppression in Mali. "They do not interfere with the wealth of any white man who dies among them . . . they simply leave it in the hands of a trustworthy white man until the one to whom it is due takes it."

Al-'Umari (pp. 54–55) described the capital of fourteenth-century Mali: "The city of BYTY is extensive in length and breadth. Its length would be about a stage and its width the same. It is not encircled by a wall and is mostly scattered. The king has several palaces enclosed by circular walls. A branch of the Nile encircles the city on all four sides."

Ibn Battuta recorded the following official titles: the royal title of *mansa*, the *farba*—a provincial governor, the *farariyya*—military commanders, the *manshaju*—the market supervisor of Iwalatan, the *dugha*—the "linguist" at the *mansa*'s court, with his companions the *jula* (singular *jali* [*dyeli* in Mande]) (Ibn Battuta p. 78) or "poets." The physical appearance of each member of the court community was governed by an elaborate dress code of rules called "sumptuary laws." In Ghana, according to al-Bakri (pp. 15–16), "among the people who follow the king's religion only he and his heir apparent (who is the son of his sister) may wear sewn clothes. All other people wear [draped] robes of cotton, silk, or brocade, according to their means." In Mali, al-ʿUmari (p. 56) was told, gold bands on the arms, neck, and ankles marked ascending military rank. Moreover, "whenever a hero adds to the list of his exploits the king gives him a pair of wide trousers, and the greater the number of a knight's exploits the bigger the size of his trousers." The king himself wore "big trousers cut out of about twenty pieces which none but he wears." Each monarch possessed a variety of insignia that marked his royal role. In Kawkaw, according to al-Bakri (p. 22), "when a king ascends the throne he is handed a signet ring, a sword, and a copy of the Koran which, as they assert, were sent to them by [the Caliph]." Al-Idrisi (p. 32) describes a very large gold nugget that belonged to the king of Ghana: "it is one of those curious objects which no one else possesses and which is not permissible for anyone else." Al-ʿUmari (p. 58) reported many examples of royal insignia, one being the flags that accompanied Mansa Musa: "standards are unfurled over him whenever he rides on horseback; they are very big flags."

Many rules served to isolate the person of the king from contact with the mundane. Concerning the king of Kawkaw, for example, al-Muhallabi (p. 8) reported: "in his own town he has a palace which nobody inhabits with him or has resort to except a eunuch slave." The Zaghawa of Kanim, he added (p. 70), "imagine that [their king] does not eat any food. There are people who have charge of this food secretly and bring it to his house. It is not known where it is brought from and if it happens that one of his subjects meets the camels carrying his provisions, he is killed instantly on the spot. He drinks his beverage in the presence of his select companions . . . Their religion is the worship of their kings, for they believe that they bring life and death, sickness and health." The same monarch, in the opinion of al-ʿUmari (p. 51), "shows an inconceivable arrogance . . . . He is veiled from his people. None sees him save at the two festivals, when he is seen at dawn and in the afternoon. During the rest of the year nobody, not even the commander-in-chief, speaks to him except from behind a screen." In Borno, Ibn Battuta (pp. 87–88) confirmed, the king "does not appear to the people and does not address them except from behind a curtain." Restrictions on royal eating in public were commonplace. In Kawkaw, according to al-Bakri (pp. 21–22), "when their king sits down [to partake of a meal] a drum is beaten, and Sudanese women dance with their thick hair flowing, and nobody in the town goes about his business until he has finished his repast, the remnants of which are thrown into the Nile. At this [the courtiers] shout boisterously so that people will know that the king has finished his meal." In fourteenth century Mali, according to the evidence of an Egyptian official who attended Mansa Musa during his visit to Cairo (al-ʿUmari p. 59), the king "does not eat in the presence of anybody . . . but eats always alone."

Even when a king held public court, communication with him passed only through an intermediary court official, as observed by Ibn Battuta in Mali (p. 74). An official at the foreign court of Egypt told al-ʿUmari (p. 61) that the visiting king of Mali "addressed me . . . only through an interpreter despite his perfect ability to speak in the Arabic tongue." Even abroad, the king remained a man apart.

In Ghana, according to al-Bakri (p. 16), "when the people who profess the same religion as the king approach him they fall on their knees

and sprinkle dust on their heads, for this is their way of greeting him."
The people of the Sudan, wrote Ibn Battuta (p. 75), "are the humblest of
people before their king and the most submissive towards him." This is
further elaborated by al-ʿUmari (pp. 56–57); "if the king [of Mali]
bestows a favor upon a person or makes him a fair promise or thanks him
for some deed the person who has received the favor grovels before him
from one end of the room to the other. When he reaches there the slaves
of the recipient of the favor or some of his friends take some of the ashes
which are always kept ready at the far end of the audience chamber for
the purpose and scatter it over the head of the favored one, who then
returns grovelling until he arrives before the king." Even Malian diplo-
mats abroad preserved this custom, according to Ibn Battuta's scribe Ibn
Juzzay (p. 76). Ibn Khaldun confirmed this (pp. 99–100). "Nobody may
enter the abode of this king save barefooted, whoever he may be," wrote
al-ʿUmari (pp. 55–56). "Whoever sneezes while the king is holding court
is severely beaten and he permits nobody to do so. But if a sneeze comes
to anyone he lies down face to the ground to sneeze so that no one may
know of it. As for the king, if he sneezes all those present beat their
breasts with their hands." In the kingdom of Kanim, according to *al-
Khabar* (p. 108), when the king sat in state "his subjects make obeisance
to him and fall on their faces."

International Relations:
Sudanic Kingdoms, the Berbers of the Sahara, Morocco, and Egypt

The powerful Sanhaja ruler of Awdaghust, in the middle of the tenth century, ruled over many tribes of the southern Sahara. The king of Ghana
"was then the wealthiest king on the face of earth because of his treasures
and stocks of gold." But he and the ruler of Kugha "stand in pressing need
of the kings of Awdaghust, because of the salt which comes from the
lands of Islam" (Ibn Hawqal p. 5).

Less than a century later, according to al-Bakri (p. 12), the same king of Awdaghust extended his authority over twenty kings of the Sudan, and even interfered in an internal warfare between two Sudanic rulers. But by the middle of the eleventh century, the balance of power changed and the people of Awdaghust recognized the authority of the ruler of Ghana (al-Bakri p. 13).

In 1054 the Almoravids conquered Awdaghust (al-Bakri p. 12). In 1076, according to al-Zuhri (p. 25), the people of Ghana became Muslims. Though al-Zuhri dates the conversion to the time of the Almoravids, it is not known in what way the Almoravids contributed to the conversion of Ghana

Yaqut's account (p. 40) of the king of Zafun related to the second quarter of the twelfth century, when the Almoravids were weakened by the rise of the Almohads. The veiled people of the Sahara acknowledged the superiority of the king of Zafun, a Sudanic ruler in the Sahel at the desert-edge. When the king of Zafun visited Marrakesh the Almoravid ruler "met him on foot, whereas the king of Zafun did not dismount for him."

On the connection between diplomatic and commercial relations we learn from al-Sarakhsi (p. 38). Around 1200 the governor of Sijilmasa wrote to "the king of the Sudan in Ghana . . . : '. . . We have heard about the imprisonment of poor traders and their being prevented from going freely about their business. The coming to and fro of merchants to a country is of benefit to its inhabitants and a help to keeping it populous. If we wished we would imprison the people of that region who happen to be in our territory but we do not think it right to do that.'" In order to keep the routes open and safe, according to the same source, the governor of Sijilmasa beheaded highway bandits who attacked caravans on their way from Sijilmasa to Ghana.

According to al-ʿUmari (p. 65), the Berbers of Air and Tadmekka were independent both of Morocco and Mali. But according to Ibn

Khaldun (pp. 94, 97) the "desert regions known as the land of the veiled men" are subject to the sultan of Mali, and Mansa Musa's authority in the desert extended as far as the vicinity of Wargala in the northern Sahara.

In the thirteenth century, according to Ibn Saʿid (pp. 44–45), Kanim expanded northwards into the Sahara as far as Kawar and Fazzan. But the power of Kanim deteriorated because of internal dissensions, which forced the royal court to be relocated to Borno. In 1391 the king of Borno, ʿUthman ibn Idris, wrote to Barquq, the Mamluk sultan of Egypt, concerning harassment by Arab nomads, who captured slaves including the king's own relatives. These slaves were sold to Egyptian merchants, and the king of Borno asked the Egyptian sultan to return the enslaved people (al-Qalqashandi p. 103).

In the fourteenth century relations between Mali and Egypt became closer because of the royal pilgrimages that passed through Cairo. The most important pilgrimage was that of Mansa Musa in 1324. There are several versions of the embarrassing situation during the encounter between Mansa Musa and the Mamluk sultan, when the visitor was expected "to kiss the ground and the sultan's hand" (al-ʿUmari pp. 61–62; compare Ibn Kathir p. 114; al-Maqrizi 116–17; Ibn Hajar al-ʿAsqalani p. 119). The Mamluk sultan gave Mansa Musa robes of honor and provided him with supplies for the journey to Mecca. Mansa Musa rewarded the sultan and his courtiers with rich presents of gold (al-ʿUmari 62; Ibn Khaldun p. 91; Ibn al-Dawadari p. 113; al-Maqrizi p. 116; Ibn Hajar al-ʿAsqalani pp. 119–20).

Diplomatic relations between Morocco and Mali began, according to Ibn Khaldun (pp. 95, 99–101), when the king of Morocco wanted to be like "the mightiest monarchs and adopt their customs in exchanging gifts with their peers and counterparts and dispatching emissaries to distant kings and far frontiers. In his time the king of Mali was the greatest of the kings of the Sudan." Ibn Khaldun then describes the exchange of embassies between Mali and Morocco.

African Economic and Exchange Systems

Towards the end of the ninth century al-Yaʿqubi (pp. 2–3) described the two major Trans-Saharan routes. One was an eastern route from Zawila to Lake Chad, famous for its slave trade. (The slave trade on this route is also described by al-Bakri [p. 10]). The other was the western route from Sijilmasa to "Ghust," meaning Awdaghust in the southwestern Sahara. At that time the eastern route seems to have been more important because al-Yaʿqubi listed the nations of the Sudan from east to west. There was also a direct route from the oases of Egypt to Ghana. But this route was closed because of sandstorms in the second half of the ninth century (Ibn Hawqal p. 5). By the tenth century the western route became far more important. The size of the trade between Sijilmasa and Awdaghust was demonstrated by the warrant Ibn Hawqal saw in Sijilmasa (pp. 4–5).

In Awdaghust, according to al-Muhallabi (p. 7), "there are excellent markets . . . and it is one of the most important metropolises, and there is a continual flow of traffic toward it from every land." Al-Bakri (p. 11) described the markets of Awdaghust: "their transactions are in gold . . . . The market there is at all times full of people so that owing to the great crowd and the noise of voices it is almost impossible for a man to hear the words of one sitting beside him." The people of Awdaghust "enjoy extensive benefits and huge wealth . . . There are handsome buildings and fine houses."

Arabic sources testify abundantly to the presence of a flourishing West African market economy. Typically, each community produced its own staple food. The Saharan folk, as al-ʿUmari (p. 65) says, "live, as desert dwellers do, on meat and milk; grain is very scarce with them." Thus communities found it advantageous to exchange the abundant products of their homes for the less accessible ones of neighbors who lived in contrasting ecological zones, or who possessed unusual natural resources. As Ibn Saʿid (p. 43) said of the Atlantic coastal folk of Awlil, "its people live on fish and turtles and their trade is in salt. They carry it by ship up to the countries on the banks of the Nile."

Economic activities on the desert edge were of great importance. Kings of the Sudan, in spite of their wealth in gold, stood "in pressing need of [the goodwill of] the kings of Awdaghust because of the salt which comes to them from the lands of Islam. They cannot do without salt." (Ibn Hawqal p. 5) The nomads, on the other hand, depended on imports of grain from the south, as reported by al-Bakri (p. 11): "sorghum and other grains are imported for them from the land of the Sudan."

The traveler Ibn Battuta (pp. 69–70) offered a vivid image of his own experience with local exchange. As he and his companions entered a settlement at the end of the day he would be greeted by women eager to trade; "each night we stayed in a village and bought what we were in need of in the way of wheat and butter for salt, spices and glass trinkets." The traveler elsewhere explained that these trinkets were called *nazm*, and that scents and spices were particularly welcome. "What pleases them most," he concluded, "are cloves, mastic, and *tasarghant*, which is their incense." As these vignettes reveal, the commerce of the Sudan often employed currencies in kind rather than coins. "For money the inhabitants of Sila use sorghum, salt, copper rings and lengths of fine cotton which they call *shakkiyyat*." (al-Bakri p. 13) "The people of the region of Kawkaw trade with salt which serves as their currency. This salt is obtained from an underground mine at Tutak, in Berber country, and transported to Tadmekka and thence to Kawkaw" (al-Bakri p. 22). The people of Kawkaw, according to Ibn Battuta (p. 87), "conduct their buying and selling with cowries, like the people of Mali." Al-ʿUmari (p. 61) confirms that in Mali the currency "consists of cowries and the merchants whose principal import these are make big profits on them." The cowrie shells came from the Maldive Islands of the Indian Ocean, and changed many hands until they reached *bilad al-sudan*. It is likely that cowries were adopted as a common currency only about the thirteenth century.

The currency of the people of Kanim "is a cloth which they weave, called *dandi*. Every piece is ten cubits long. They make purchases with it from a quarter of a cubit upwards. They also use cowries, beads, copper in round pieces, and coined silver as currency, but all valued in terms of that cloth." (al-ʿUmari p. 52) In the detailed description of the copper mine in Takedda, Ibn Battuta (p. 87) also described the use of copper as currency: "When they have smelted it into red copper they make bars of it a span and a half long, some thin and some thick, of which the thick are sold at 400 bars per gold mithqal and the thin at 600 or 700 for a mithqal. This is their currency. With the thin ones they buy meat and firewood and with the thick ones male and female slaves, sorghum, butter, and wheat."

Ultimately, however, these Sudanic media of exchange could also be understood in relation to units of gold, and it was through the idiom of gold that both medieval Islamic merchants and Arabic writers converted West African values into those of the Mediterranean world. In the desert town of Tadmekka, they minted their own coins, but these remained mere ingots of precious metal. "Their dinars," wrote al-Bakri (p. 21), "are called 'bald' because they are pure gold without any stamp."

In principle a *dinar*, the gold coin of the Islamic world, should weigh 4.25 grams, and could also be considered a unit of weight called a *mithqal*. A standard *dirham*, or a silver coin, should weigh 2.97 grams, or seven-tenths of a *mithqal*, and ten or twelve of them should be worth one *dinar*. In practice, however, there were many reasons why merchants in different places at various times, or even individual rulers, might wish to change these values, so that in fact what appears to be a precise information found in the sources must be considered at best approximate. The same warning applies to the *uqiyya* and *ratl*, or Islamic ounce and pound, and to the *qintar*, a larger unit of weight comprised of 100 *ratls*. Another measurement of distance, "the stage" or a day's journey, was obviously very elastic.

Each kingdom possessed a distinctive array of exportable resources, much of which the king sought to gather to himself through taxation. Al-Muhallabi (pp. 7–8) describes the treasures of two contemporary kingdoms. In Kawkaw "the wealth of the people of his country consists of livestock. The king's treasure-houses are spacious, his treasure consisting principally of salt." The Zaghawa king of Kanim, according to the same source, was differently endowed, for "his wealth consists of livestock such as sheep, cattle, camels, and horses."

Sudanic kings obtained slaves for export from two sources. Very important were their judicial systems, for the threat of enslavement was a significant instrument of social control. Sometimes it was said, as al-Ya'qubi reported (p. 3), that kings sold their own subjects "without any pretext or war," but probably the situation described by al-Bakri (p. 14) in Sila was more typical. There, enslavement was a punishment for certain misdeeds; for example, "a person who falls victim to a thief may either sell or kill him, as he chooses." Judicial pretext, however, did not suffice to generate enough slaves to satisfy the eager medieval Mediterranean market. Slave raiding was important in the economy of the kingdoms of the Sudan. Sudanic kings routinely used their military forces to raid their neighbors in order to seize slaves. Al-Zuhri (p. 25) explained the inferiority of the victims of slave raiding: "These people [the Barbara and Amima] have no iron and fight only with clubs of ebony. For this reason the people of Ghana overcome them, for they fight them with swords and spears." Similarly, according to al-Idrisi (p. 30), "the people of Barisa, Sila and Ghana make forays into the land of Lamlam and capture its inhabitants. They bring them to their own countries and sell them to the visiting merchants. The latter export them to all the countries." The Muslim king of Kanim, according to Ibn Sa'id (p. 44), "often makes raids from there with his fleet on the lands of the pagans on the shores of this lake and attacks their ships and kills and takes prisoners."

It was West African gold, however, that attracted the greatest interest in the outside world. "[The king of] Ghana," wrote Ibn Hawqal (p. 5), "is the wealthiest king on the face of the earth because of his treasures and stocks of gold extracted in olden times for his predecessors and himself." The king of Ghana claimed all the nuggets above a certain size for himself, explained al-Bakri (p. 17), "only the gold dust being left for the people. But for this the people would accumulate gold until it lost its value."

Some gold was obtained by seasonal panning from alluvial deposits, explained al-Idrisi (pp. 33–34); "they search as long as the Nile is receding, each one finding there what God, praise be unto him, allows, whether a large or a small quantity of gold, none being completely disappointed. When the Nile has returned to its level [at the end of the annual rainy season], these people sell whatever gold has fallen into their hands, trading with each other. Most of the gold is bought by the people of Wargala and Morocco, who export it to the mints in their own country, where *dinars* are struck from it, which they use in trade. . . . This is the greatest source of income for the Sudan, upon which both great and small rely."

In other cases, al-ʿUmari learned (p. 64), gold was mined; "the gold is extracted by digging pits about a man's height in depth and the gold is found embedded in the sides of the pits or sometimes collected at the bottom of them." Mansa Musa explained to Ibn Amir Hajib, who in his turn told al-ʿUmari (p. 58): "gold was his prerogative and he collected the crop as a tribute except for what the people of that country took by theft." The king of Mali regarded his subjects as those "whom he simply employs in extracting the gold from its deposits."

In the eleventh century al-Bakri (p. 18) identified the merchants who "export gold to other countries" as the Banu Naghmarata, "who speak an unintelligible language." These merchants were the Wangara, the itinerary traders of the Western Sudan, and their "unintelligible language" was one of the Mande dialects. Al-Idrisi used the term Wangara to refer both to "the country of gold, famous on account of its good quality and abundance" (pp. 33–34), and to the traders. Hence, Tiraqqa was "one of the towns of Wangara" (p. 34), though it was not part of the land of gold, but an important market where "the people of Ghana and Tadmekka assemble" (al-Bakri p. 20). Ibn Battuta (p. 70) referred to the Wanjarata as "traders of the Sudan." Religion too played an important role in defining the identity of the Wangara commercial diaspora; as the thirteenth-century writer Ibn Sa'id (Levtzion and Hopkins, *Corpus*, p. 186) recognized, the Wangara were the black people "among whom Islam spread [most] widely."

Mansa Musa told his informants (al-'Umari p. 54) that the non-Muslims "bring gold dust to him each year. They are uncouth infidels. If the sultan wished he could extend his authority over them but the kings of this kingdom have learned by experience that as soon as one of them conquers one of the gold towns and Islam spreads and the muezzin calls to prayer there the gold begins to decrease and then disappears, while it increases in the neighboring heathen countries. When they had learned the truth of this by experience they left the gold countries under the control of the heathen people and were content with their vassalage and the tribute imposed upon them." Some years after the Malian emperor's visit to Cairo al-'Umari (p. 58) weighed two contradictory statements. One was by Ibn Amir Hajib, who was told by Mansa Musa that gold in principle belonged to him. The other statement was by "the truthful and trustworthy Shaykh Abu 'Uthman Sa'id al-Dukkali, who lived at BYTY [capital of Mali] for 35 years and went to and fro in this kingdom." He reported that the king of Mali "is given only a part of it as a present by way of gaining his favor, and he makes a profit on the sale of it, for they have none in their country." Al-'Umari concludes, "What al-Dukkali says is more reliable."

The wealth accumulated by a Sudanic king through the collection of tribute at home and trade abroad was largely destined for redistribution among his court officials and other worthy notables. This aspect of royal policy was best articulated by al-'Umari (p. 56): "among their chiefs are some whose wealth derived from the king reaches 50,000 *mithqal*s of gold every year, besides which he keeps them in horses and clothes. His whole ambition is to give them fine clothes and to make his towns into cities." The spectacular generosity of Mansa Musa during his pilgrimage attracted foreign dignitaries to Mali. But Ibn Battuta (p. 72) was greatly disappointed by the small gift he received from Mansa Sulayman, Mansa Musa's brother.

Al-Idrisi (p. 29) described a typical exchange: "the people of Morocco go there with wool, copper and beads, and they export from there gold and slaves." Only royals were able to import horses. "The king of this country," wrote al-ʿUmari (p. 56) of Mali, "imports Arab horses and pays high prices for them." In Egypt, says Ibn al-Dawadari (p. 112), the Sudanese pilgrims discovered that "there was no limit to the different commodities in this country [Egypt] and they saw every day something better than the last." Members of the upper classes imported white slaves, mainly Arab females and Turkish males (al-ʿUmari p. 55; Ibn Battuta p. 86; al-Maqrizi p. 116).

Sudanic governments had a reputation for probity and were known to respect the property rights of foreigners (Ibn Battuta pp. 81–82). Trade was encouraged by the security of the roads and the justice administered against oppression by officials (Ibn Battuta pp. 69, 81–82). The fullest account of the trans-Saharan trade in the thirteenth century was recorded in 1356 by Lisan al-Din Ibn al-Khatib (1313–1375) (pp. 48–49) in his native Granada, when Muhammad, a great-grandson of one of the enterprising Maqqari brothers named Abu Bakr, visited this town. The Maqqari family operated a sophisticated commercial enterprise that extended from Tlemcen near the Mediterranean to Sijilmasa and Walata. "They established the desert route by digging wells and seeing to the security of merchants. They introduced the drum as a starting signal and the standard which was carried in front while the caravan was on the move . . . . They acquired properties and houses in those regions, married wives and begat children by concubines." When Mali conquered Walata, the Maqqari brother resident in Walata "entered into relations with the king, who made him welcome and enabled him to trade in all his country, addressing him as a dear and sincere friend. Then the king began to correspond with those [brothers] in Tlemcen, seeking from them the accomplishment of his desires and addressing them in similar terms."

Walata was the first town of Mali that Ibn Battuta (p. 68) entered from the desert. In addition to the governor *(farba)* the king of Mali was represented by the *mushrif*, the commercial supervisor. The foreign merchants came to pay him their respects and received reception-gifts from him.

Both in Walata and in the capital of Mali, Ibn Battuta (pp. 68, 71) wrote in advance to a local resident, a white man who originated from north of the Sahara. It seems that these hosts were also middlemen and brokers. According to Ibn Khaldun's informants (p. 97), "the capital of the people of Mali is an extensive place with cultivated land fed by running water, very populous with brisk markets. At present it is a station for trading caravans from the Maghrib, Ifriqiya, and Egypt, and goods are imported from all parts." One caravan approaching it through Tadmekka, he was told, had no less than 12,000 camels.

As foreign merchants established themselves in many parts of the Sudan, great markets flourished at major towns. In Kawkaw, according to al-Muhallabi (p. 8), "there are markets and trading houses . . . to which there is continuous traffic from all parts." In Kawkaw, al-Idrisi (p. 35) says, "the nobles and eminent persons . . . mix with the merchants, sit in their company, and take shares in their wares, [participating in the profit] by way of *muqarada*."

Muqarada or *qirad* is a commercial arrangement in which an investor or group of investors entrusts capital or merchandise to an agent-manager, who is to trade with it and then return it to the investor with the principal and previously agreed-upon share of the profits. As a reward for his labor, the agent receives the remaining share of the profits. However, in case of a loss resulting from an unsuccessful business venture, the agent is in no way liable for the return of the lost investment. He loses his expended time, effort, and anticipated share of the profit, while it is the investor who exclusively bears the direct financial loss. This Islamic commercial arrangement was introduced to the Italian seaports in the tenth or eleventh centuries, and became known as *commenda*—one of the many intriguing links created by Arab merchants between the Mediterranean world and Africa south of the Sahara.

* * *

This analysis has not exhausted the evidence that can be drawn from those texts on these and other themes. Students of African history are invited to explore the texts, and as different readers will have their own interpretations of the sources, the result will be a more meaningful and multifaceted history of the early kingdoms of West Africa, of the initial phases in the spread of Islam, of emerging patterns of trade, and of other topics that are not dealt with in this introductory essay.

1. Kingdoms of Habasha and the Sudan with a Description of Two Trans-Saharan Trade Routes

AL-YA'QUBI (872-890)

Al-Ya'qubi traveled to many parts of the Islamic world. He wrote his book of history (Tarikh) in 872 when he was in Khurasan, in present-day Iran. His account of peoples and kingdoms provides the earliest insight into the political history and the dynamics of state building in West Africa. Among the names he mentions, only three kingdoms, known from other sources, are identifiable today: Kanim, Kawkaw, and Ghana. Kanim was then the kingdom of Zaghawa. Kawkaw (Gao) and Ghana had already developed into large-scale states, within which lesser subordinate kings paid allegiance to a supreme high ruler.

The Kingdoms of the Habasha and the Sudan

When the progeny of Nuh dispersed from the country of Babylon, the descendants of Ham son of Nuh went to the West . . . .

After they had crossed the Nile of Egypt, the descendants of Kush son of Ham, namely the Habasha and the Sudan, split into two groups. One of these groups proceeded to the south, between the east and the west. These were the Nuba, Buja, Habasha and Zanj. The other group went to the west. These were the Zaghawa, HBSH, Qaqu, Marawiyyun, Maranda, Kawkaw and Ghana.

The Sudan who went to the west traversed several countries and cre-

Source: N. Levtzion and J.F.P. Hopkins, *Corpus of Early Arabic Sources for West African History* (Princeton: Markus Wiener Publishers, 2000 and 2006), pp. 21–22.

1

ated several kingdoms. The first of their kingdoms is that of the Zaghawa who live in the place called Kanim. Their dwellings are huts made of reeds and they have no towns. Their king is called KAKRH. Among the Zaghawa is a group called the HWDN who have a king who is from among the Zaghawa . . . .

Then there is the kingdom of Kawkaw, which is the greatest of the realms of the Sudan, the most important and powerful. All the kingdoms obey its king. Kawkaw is the name of the town. Besides this there are a number of kingdoms whose rulers pay allegiance to him and acknowledge his sovereignty, although they are kings in their own lands . . . .

Then there is the kingdom of Ghana, whose king is also very powerful. In his country are the gold mines, and under his authority are a number of kings. Among these are the kingdom of ʿAM and the kingdom of Sama. Gold is found in the whole of this country.

Al-Yaʿqubi wrote his work of geography, "The Book of Countries" (Kitab al-Buldan), *in 889 or 890 while he was living in Egypt. Al-Yaʿqubi described the two major trans-Saharan routes. One was an eastern route from Zawila to Lake Chad, famous for its slave trade. The other was the western route from Sijilmasa to "Ghust," meaning Awdaghust in the southwestern Sahara. At the end of the ninth century, according to al-Yaʿqubi, its king "had no religion or law," meaning that he was not a Muslim.*

Zawila

Beyond Waddan to the south is the town of Zawila. Its people are Muslims, all of them Ibadis, and they go on pilgrimage to Mecca . . . .

They export black slaves from among the . . . peoples of the Sudan, because they live close to Zawila, whose people capture them. I have been informed that the kings of the Sudan sell their [own] people without any pretext or war . . . .

Fifteen days' journey beyond Zawila is a town called Kawar, inhabited by Muslims from various tribes, most of them Berbers. It is they who bring in the Sudan [as slaves]. . . .

He who travels from Sijilmasa toward the south, making for the land of the Sudan (which is inhabited by different tribes of the Sudan), goes through the desert for a distance of fifty stages. Then he will meet in the desert a people called Anbiya, belonging to the Sanhaja, who have no permanent dwellings. It is their custom to veil their faces with their turbans. They do not wear [sewn] clothes, but wrap themselves in lengths of cloth. They subsist on camels, for they have no crops, wheat or otherwise. Then the traveler will reach a town called Ghust [Awdaghust], which is in an inhabited valley with dwellings. It is the residence of their king, who has no religion or law. He raids the land of the Sudan, who have many kingdoms.

2. The Saharan Gold Trade from Egypt to Ghana via the Maghrib and Awdaghust

IBN HAWQAL (947-951)

Ibn Hawqal, a native of Upper Mesopotamia, traveled in the Maghrib and in Spain during the years 947–51. He visited Sijilmasa in 951; there he saw a promissory note for 42,000 gold dinars in the possession of a man named Abu Ishaq Ibrahim. The debtor, named Muhammad b. Saʿdun, was a trader from Sijilmasa who was living at that time in Awdaghust. Abu Ishaq Ibrahim the creditor also used to travel between Sijilmasa and Awdaghust, and it was from him that Ibn Hawqal recorded information concerning Awdaghust and its relations with the kingdoms of the Sudan. In the middle of the tenth century a powerful Sanhaja king ruled Awdaghust. At that time, according to Ibn Hawqal, the king of Ghana was very wealthy, but he depended upon [the goodwill of] the rulers of Awdaghust because his land needed salt that came to them from the lands of Islam to the north.

The Berbers of the Maghrib are divided into tribes of which the number cannot be counted precisely. . . . They have kings, chiefs, and tribal headmen whom they obey without question; these kings give commands and are not disobeyed. Their property consists of great herds of livestock. Among those living apart deep in the deserts are the Sanhaja of Awdaghust. I heard from Abu Ishaq Ibrahim b. ʿAbd Allah, nicknamed "Faragh Shughluh" (His Work is Done), who was the creditor and the

Source: N. Levtzion and J.F.P. Hopkins, *Corpus of Early Arabic Sources for West African History.* (Princeton: Markus Wiener Publishers, 2000 and 2006), pp. 48–49, 51–52.

owner of the warrant [promissory note] which I have mentioned in [connection with] Awdaghust, that Tinbarutan b. Usfayshar, king of all the Sanhaja, told him that he had been ruling over them for twenty years, and that each year people came to visit him whom he had never known before, nor heard of, nor set eyes on. He said that there were about 300,000 tents, including shelters and huts, and that the kingship over his tribe had always been in his family . . . .

This king of Awdaghust maintains relations with the ruler of Ghana. [The king of] Ghana is the wealthiest king on the face of the earth because of his treasures and stocks of gold extracted in olden times for his predecessors and himself. He sends gifts to the ruler of Kugha (although Kugha does not approach the ruler of Ghana in opulence and well-being) and they sent gifts to him. They stand in pressing need of [the goodwill of] the kings of Awdaghust because of the salt which comes to them from the lands of Islam. They cannot do without this salt, of which one load, in the interior and more remote parts of the land of the Sudan, may fetch between 200 and 300 dinars.

From the back of the oases they used to journey to the land of the Sudan and the Maghrib on the road which was traveled of old from Egypt to Ghana, but it was cut off . . . From Upper Egypt on the frontier of the Nuba to the oases takes about three days in a desert that constitutes the frontier. Nubian and Egyptian travelers used continually to proceed to the Maghrib and the land of the Sudan by more than one road across deserts and this did not cease till the days of the rule of Abu'l-ʿAbbas Ahmad Ibn Tulun. They had a way to the Fezzan and Barqa but it went out of use because of what happened to the caravans in several years when the winds overwhelmed them with sand and more than one caravan perished. Abu'l-ʿAbbas ordered the road to be closed and forbade anyone to go out on it.

3. Islamic and Pre-Islamic Customs of the Berber, Zaghawa, and Kawkaw Peoples

AL-MUHALLABI (c. 970-990)

Al-Hassan b. Muhammad al-Misri al-Muhallabi, who died in 990, wrote a geographical work that became known as the Kitab al-ʿAziz *or* al-ʿAzizi *because it was dedicated to the Fatimid Caliph al-ʿAziz (r. 976–96). The Fatimids controlled much of the trade of North Africa and the Sahara in the tenth century, and al-Muhallabi was able to record precious information about religion and politics in the contemporary kingdoms of West Africa. Al-Muhallabi's work was lost, but some fragments survived as quotations in the work of Yaqut, who wrote between 1212 and 1229.*

Al-Muhallabi reports that the people of Awdaghust had become Muslims. As an Ismaʿili, patronized by the Fatimid Caliph, al-Muhallabi attributed the conversion of the people of Awdaghust to the Mahdi ʿUbayd Allah (r. 909–34), founder of the Fatimid dynasty. There is no evidence, however, that the Mahdi ever extended his authority far into the desert. Rather, most of the people of Awdaghust in the tenth century were Ibadis.

In the account of al-Muhallabi as in al-Yaʿqubi, Kanim is the kingdom of the Zaghawa. Al-Muhallabi vividly describes how they worship their kings, an example of what modern anthropologists would call "divine kingship." Al-Muhallabi provides the earliest description of a capital of a kingdom of the Sudan, Kawkaw (Gao), with two towns, one of which was the commercial town. He also provides the earliest account of the progress of Islam into the lands of the Sudan. The king of Kawkaw, he

Source: N. Levtzion and J.F.P. Hopkins, *Corpus of Early Arabic Sources for West African History* (Princeton: Markus Wiener Publishers, 2000 and 2006), pp. 168–74.

*wrote, "pretends before his subjects to be a Muslim, and most of them
pretend to be Muslims too."*

Al-Muhallabi says: Awdaghust is a town between two mountains
deep inland, 40-odd stages to the south of Sijilmasa, through sands and
arid wastes, with known water-points. On some of these are tents of the
Berbers. There are excellent markets in Awdaghust, and it is one of the
most important metropolises, and there is a continual flow of traffic
toward it from every land. Its people are Muslims, who recite the Koran,
study Islamic jurisprudence, and possess mosques and oratories. They
have been converted to Islam by the Mahdi ʿUbayd Allah, for previously
they were infidels who worshipped the sun, who used to eat carrion and
blood . . . .

Al-Muhallabi says: [. . . .] the kingdom of the Zaghawa is a great
kingdom among the kingdoms of the Sudan . . . . Their houses are all reed
huts as is also the palace of their king, whom they exalt and worship
instead of Allah. They imagine that he does not eat any food. There are
persons who have charge of this food secretly and bring it to his house. It
is not known where it is brought from and if it happens that one of his
subjects meets the camels carrying his provisions, he is killed instantly on
the spot. He drinks his beverage in the presence of his select companions.
This drink is made of millet fortified with honey. His attire consists of
trousers of thin wool, over which he wraps himself in excellent garments
made of a single piece of wool and *susi* silk and costly brocade. He has
unlimited authority over his subjects and enslaves from among them anyone he wants. His wealth consists of livestock such as sheep, cattle,
camels, and horses. The greater part of the crops of their country is
sorghum and cowpeas and then wheat. Most of his subjects go naked,
wrapped [only] in skins. Their means of subsistence is crops and the own-
ership of livestock. Their religion is the worship of their kings, for they
believe that they bring life and death, sickness and health . . . .

[Kawkaw is] the name of a people and a country of the Sudan. According to al-Muhallabi . . . . their king pretends before his subjects to be a Muslim and most of them pretend to be Muslims too. He has a town on the Nile, on the eastern bank, which is called Sarnah where there are markets and trading houses and to which there is continuous traffic from all parts. He has another town to the west of the Nile where he and his men and those who have his confidence live. There is a mosque there where he prays but the communal prayer-ground is between the two towns. In his own town he has a palace which nobody inhabits with him or has resort to except a eunuch slave.

They are all Muslims. The costume of their king and his chief companions consists of shirts and turbans. They ride horses barebacked. His kingdom is more populous than that of the Zaghawa but the land of the Zaghawa is more extensive. The wealth of the people of his country consists of livestock. The king's treasure-houses are spacious, his treasure consisting principally of salt.

4. Awdaghust Falls to the Almoravids, Ghana at Its Height, Notes on Neighboring Lands

AL-BAKRI (1068)

Abu ʿUbayd ʿAbd Allah b. ʿAbd al-ʿAziz al-Bakri, who died at an advanced age in 1094, is by far the most important source for West African history until the fourteenth century. He lived most of his life in Cordova and Almeria, and seems never to have left Islamic Spain. His major geographical work, which he wrote in 1068, is based on information he gathered from merchants and other visitors to the lands of the Sudan beyond the Sahara. Al-Bakri had an inquisitive and methodical mind. By the skillful combination of written and oral sources he presented a dynamic account of the Western Sudan during one of the more crucial periods of its history. It was when the trans-Saharan trade expanded and the kingdoms of Ghana, Takrur and Gao reached the height of their power. Al-Bakri quoted from the lost work of the tenth-century geographer Muhammad b. Yusuf al-Warraq (904–973). He also borrowed information from Ibn Hawqal concerning the king of Awdaghust in the mid-tenth century. According to al-Bakri this ruler raided a kingdom of the Sudan when he came to the aid of his ally, another king of the Sudan. The passage on the Damdam, who eat men and go on pilgrimage to a huge idol in the form of a woman, is borrowed from the book Akhbar al-Zaman, attributed to al-Masʿudi (d. 956). Al-Bakri recorded events close to the time of writing: the conversion of the king of Takrur in 1040, the rise of the Almoravid movement in 1048 and their conquest of Awdaghust in

Source: N. Levtzion and J.F.P. Hopkins, *Corpus of Early Arabic Sources for West African History* (Princeton: Markus Wiener Publishers, 2000 and 2006), pp. 63–87.

1054, and the succession of a new king to the throne of Ghana in 1063. According to al-Bakri, Awdaghust recognized the authority of the king of Ghana for some time in the first half of the tenth century. The accuracy of al-Bakri's account may be tested by an exceptionally detailed description of the course of the Niger River (which he called the "Nile") as it penetrates northward into the Sahara, and then turns back to the south.

Al-Bakri provides evidence for patterns of Islamization in the three contemporary kingdoms of Ghana, Takrur, and Gao (Kawkaw). In the capitals of the three kingdoms there were special quarters for Muslim residents. In Ghana the king and commoners remained loyal to their ancestral religion. In Gao the king was a Muslim but pre-Islamic customs persisted. In Takrur the Muslim king forced Islam on his subjects, and even waged a holy war against his neighbors. One may suggest that these three patterns represent three stages in the development of Islam, with Ghana as the earliest phase and Takrur the last phase. Gao represents the kind of Islam that prevailed in most West African kingdoms at least until the eighteenth century. Al-Bakri also describes the events that led to the conversion of a king by a Muslim, whose prayer to Allah had saved his country from a severe drought. Al-Bakri's brief reference to Kanim, that "scarcely anyone reaches," suggests that in the middle of the eleventh century this kingdom was still rather isolated and had not yet been converted to Islam.

Zawila lies between the *maghrib* [west] and the *qibla* [east] from Tripoli [that is, due south of Tripoli]. From there slaves are exported to Ifriqiya [Tunisia] and other neighboring regions. They are bought for short pieces of red cloth. Forty stages lie between Zawila and the region of Kanim. The Kanimis live beyond the desert of Zawila and scarcely anybody reaches them. They are pagan Sudan. Some assert that there is a people there descended from the Banu Umayya, who found their way there during their persecution by the Abbasids. They still preserve the dress and customs of the Arabs . . . .

Then [there is a route from Morocco southward] to Awdaghust, which is a large town, populous and built on sandy ground, overlooked by a large mountain, completely barren and devoid of vegetation.

In Awdaghust there is one cathedral mosque and many smaller ones, all well attended. In all the mosques there are teachers of the Koran. Around the town are gardens with date palms. Wheat is grown there, by digging with hoes, and it is watered with buckets. Only the kings and the rich eat wheat there; the rest of the people eat sorghum. Excellent cucumbers grow there, and there are a few small fig trees and some vines, as well as plantations of henna that produce a large crop.

Awdaghust possesses wells with sweet water. Cattle and sheep are so numerous that for a *mithqal* one may buy ten rams or more. Honey too is very abundant, brought from the land of the Sudan. The people of Awdaghust enjoy extensive benefits and huge wealth. The market there is at all times full of people, so that owing to the great crowd and the noise of voices it is almost impossible for a man to hear the words of one sitting beside him. Their transactions are in gold, and they have no silver. There are handsome buildings and fine houses. It is a country where the inhabitants have yellow complexions because they suffer from fevers and splenitis. There is hardly anyone who does not complain of one or the other. Wheat, dates, and raisins are imported to Awdaghust from the domains of Islam despite the great distance. The price of wheat is most of the time six *mithqal*s for a hundredweight, and the price for dates and raisins is the same.

Most of the inhabitants of Awdaghust are natives of Ifriqiya, members of [such tribes as the] Barqajana, Nafusa, Lawata, Zanata, and Nafzawa, but there are also a few people from other countries. There are Sudan women, good cooks, one being sold for 100 *mithqal*s or more . . . .

11

. . . . The gold of Awdaghust is better and purer than that of any other people on earth.

During the decade following the year 350/961–62 the ruler of Awdaghust was Tin Yarutan b. Wisanu b. Nizar, a man of the Sanhaja whose authority was recognized by more than twenty kings of the Sudan, every one of whom paid him tribute. His domain stretched the distance of two months' traveling in length and width over inhabited country, and he could put 100,000 camelry in the field. When T'RYN the king of Masin asked him for help against the king of Awgham, Tin Yarutan came to his aid with 50,000 camelry, and they invaded, pillaging and burning the country of Awgham, whose soldiers were taken unawares. When [the king of] Awgham saw what had happened to his country, he did not care about dying; he threw down his shield, bent his leg from astride his mount and then sat on it [the shield] until Tin Yarutan's men killed him. When the women of Awgham saw his dead body they threw themselves into wells or committed suicide in other ways out of grief for him or being too proud to be possessed by white men . . . .

In the year 446/1054–55 'Abd Allah b. Yasin invaded the town of Awdaghust, a flourishing locality, a large town containing markets, numerous palms, and henna trees resembling olive trees with their large size. This town used to be the residence of the king of the Sudan who was called Ghana before the Arabs entered [the city of] Ghana. Awdaghust contains solidly erected buildings and handsome houses. It is separated from Sijilmasa by a distance of two months' marching. From Awdaghust to Ghana is fifteen days. This [former] city was inhabited by Zanata together with Arabs who were always at loggerheads with each other. They owned great riches and slaves so numerous that one person among them might possess a thousand servants or more. The Almoravids violated its women and declared everything that they took there to be the booty of the community. 'Abd Allah Yasin killed there a man called Zibaqara, a half-caste Arab from Qayrawan who was known for his piety and virtue, his diligence in reciting the Koran, and for performing the Pilgrimage. The Almoravids persecuted the people of Awdaghust only because they recognized the authority of the ruler of Ghana . . . .

A description of the land of the Sudan and its famous towns, the communications between them, the distances which separate them one from another, its curiosities and the customs of the inhabitants

The Banu Gudala, whose territory touches the land of the Sudan, live at the farthest limit of the domains of Islam. From the border of their country to Sanghana, the nearest town of the land of the Sudan, is six days' traveling. The city of Sanghana consists of two towns standing on either bank of the Nile. Its habitations reach the ocean. The town of Sanghana is close on the southwestern side to that of Takrur, situated also on the Nile. The inhabitants are Sudan, who, like all other Sudan, were previously pagans and worshipped *dakakir* (their word for idols) until Warjabi b. Rabis became their ruler. He embraced Islam, introduced among them the Islamic religious law and compelled them to observe it, thus opening their eyes to the truth. Warjabi died in the year 432/1040–41 and the people of Takrur are Muslims today.

From the town of Takrur you go to Sila. This place too consists of two towns situated on both banks of the Nile and its inhabitants are Muslims who were converted to Islam by Warjabi, may God have mercy upon him. Between Sila and the town of Ghana is a distance of twenty days' march over country inhabited by the Sudan, one tribe after another. The king of Sila is at war with the pagans among them, there being a distance of only one day's march between him and the first of them, who are the inhabitants of the town of Qalanbu. The king of Sila rules a vast kingdom with a numerous population and is almost a match for the king of Ghana. For money the inhabitants of Sila use sorghum, salt, copper rings and lengths of fine cotton that they call *shakkiyyat*. They own many cows but have no sheep or goats . . . .

. . . . The people of this country, as well as the inhabitants of the other regions of the land of the Sudan which we have mentioned, observe the law that a person who falls victim to a thief may either sell or kill him, as he chooses. Concerning the adulterer, the law is that he should be flayed alive.

From TRNQH the country inhabited by Sudan extends to the region of the Zafqu [probably the same as the Zafun of other sources]. They are a nation of Sudan who worship a certain snake, a monstrous serpent with a mane and a tail and a head shaped like that of the Bactrian camel. It lives in a cave in the desert. At the mouth of the cave stand a trellis and stones and the habitation of the adepts of the cult of that snake. They hang up precious garments and costly objects on the trellis and place plates of food and cups of milk and intoxicating drink there. When they want the serpent to come out to the trellis they pronounce certain formulas and whistle in a particular way and the snake emerges. When one of their rulers dies they assemble all those whom they regard as worthy of kingship, bring them to the cave, and pronounce known formulas. Then the snake approaches them and smells one man after another until it prods one with its nose. As soon as it has done this it turns away towards the cave. The one prodded follows as fast as he can and pulls from its tail or its mane as many hairs as he is able. His kingship will last as many years as he has hairs, one hair per year. This, they assert, is an infallible prediction . . . .

Ghana and the customs of its inhabitants

Ghana is a title given to their kings; the name of the region is Awkar, and their king today, namely in the year 460/1067–68, is Tunka Manin. He ascended the throne in 455/1063. The name of his predecessor was Basi and he became their ruler at the age of 85. He led a praiseworthy life on account of his love of justice and friendship for the Muslims. At the end of his life he became blind, but he concealed this from his subjects and pretended that he could see. When something was put before him he said: "This is good" or "This is bad." His ministers deceived the people by indicating to the king in cryptic words what he should say, so that the commoners could not understand. Basi was a maternal uncle of Tunka Manin. This is their custom and their habit, that only the son of the king's sister inherits the kingship. He has no doubt that his successor is a son of his sister, while he is not certain that his son is in fact his own, and he is not convinced of the genuineness of his relationship to him. This Tunka Manin is powerful, rules an enormous kingdom, and possesses great authority.

The city of Ghana consists of two towns situated on a plain. One of these towns, which is inhabited by Muslims, is large and possesses twelve mosques, in one of which they assemble for the Friday prayer. There are salaried imams and muezzins, as well as jurists and scholars. In the environs are wells with sweet water, from which they drink and with which they grow vegetables. The king's town is six miles distant from this one and bears the name of "The Forest." Between these two towns there are continuous habitations. The houses of the inhabitants are of stone and acacia wood. The king has a palace and a number of domed dwellings all surrounded with an enclosure like a city wall. In the king's town, and not far from his court of justice, is a mosque where the Muslims who arrive at his court pray. Around the king's town are domed buildings and groves and thickets where the sorcerers of these people, men in charge of the religious cult, live. In them too are their idols and the tombs of their kings. These woods are guarded and none may enter them and know what is there. In them also are the king's prisons. If somebody is imprisoned there no news of him is ever heard again. The king's interpreters, the official in charge of his treasury and the majority of his ministers are Muslims. Among the people who follow the king's religion only he and his heir apparent (who is the son of his sister) may wear sewn clothes. All other people wear robes of cotton, silk, or brocade, according to their means. All of them shave their beards, and women shave their heads. The king adorns himself like a woman, [wearing necklaces] around his neck and [bracelets] on his forearms, and he puts on a high cap decorated with gold and wrapped in a turban of fine cotton. He sits in audience or to hear grievances against officials in a domed pavilion around which stand ten horses covered with gold-embroidered materials. Behind the king stand ten pages holding shields and swords decorated with gold, and on his right are the sons of the [vassal] kings of his country wearing splendid garments and their hair plaited with gold. The governor of the city sits on the ground before the king and around him are ministers seated likewise. At the door of the pavilion are dogs of excellent pedigree that hardly ever leave the place where the king is, guarding him. Round their necks they wear collars of gold and silver studded with a number of balls of the same metals. The audience is announced by the beating of a drum, which they call *duba*, made from a long hollow log. When the people who profess the same religion as the king approach him they fall on their knees and sprinkle dust on their heads, for this is their way of greeting him. As for the Muslims, they greet him only by clapping their hands.

Their religion is paganism and the worship of idols. When their king dies they construct over the place where his tomb will be an enormous dome of acacia wood. Then they bring him on a bed covered with a few carpets and cushions and place him beside the dome. At his side they place his ornaments, his weapons, and the vessels from which he used to eat and drink, filled with various kinds of food and beverages. They place there too the men who used to serve his meals. They close the door of the dome and cover it with mats and furnishings. Then the people assemble, who heap earth upon it until it becomes like a big hillock and dig a ditch around it until the mound can be reached only at one place.

They make sacrifices to their dead and make offerings of intoxicating drinks.

On every donkey-load of salt when it is brought into the country their king levies one golden dinar, and two dinars when it is sent out. From a load of copper the king's due is five *mithqals*, and from a load of other goods ten *mithqals*. The best gold found in his land comes from the town of Ghiyaru, which is eighteen days' traveling distant from the king's town over a country inhabited by tribes of the Sudan whose dwellings are contiguous.

The nuggets found in all the mines of his country are reserved for the king, only this gold dust being left for the people. But for this the people would accumulate gold until it lost its value. The nuggets may weigh from an ounce to a pound. It is related that the king owns a nugget as large as a big stone.

The town of Ghiyaru is twelve miles distant from the Nile and contains many Muslims.

The countryside of Ghana is unhealthy and not populous, and it is almost impossible to avoid falling ill there during the time their crops are ripening. There is mortality among strangers at the time of the harvest.

As for the road from Ghana to Ghiyaru, it goes [first] to the town of Samaqanda, which is four days' traveling distant. The people of Samaqanda are the best archers among the Sudan. From there [one goes for] two days to the region called Taqa. Most of the trees of Taqa belong to the species called *tadmut*, which is similar to the *arak* tree save that it bears fruit like a watermelon, filled with something resembling candy of a sourish-sweet taste, which is useful for curing those sick of the fever.

From there to a channel deriving from the Nile and called Zughu it is one day's march. Camels wade through it, but people cross it only by boat. From there one goes to a region called Gharantal, a big town and [the center of a] mighty kingdom. No Muslims live there but when they enter their country the inhabitants treat them with respect and step out of their way. In that country elephants and giraffes propagate their species.

Then [the road leads] from Gharantal to Ghiyaru.

The king of Ghana, when he calls up his army, can put 200,000 men into the field, more than 40,000 of them archers. The horses in Ghana are very small. Excellent black-and-white veined ebony grows there. The inhabitants sow their crops twice yearly, the first time in the moist earth during the season of the Nile flood, and later in the earth [that has preserved its humidity].

West of Ghiyaru, on the Nile [Niger], is the town of Yarisna, inhabited by Muslims surrounded by polytheists . . . . From Yarisna the Sudan who speak an unintelligible language, called the Banu Naghmarata, who are merchants, export gold to other countries.

On the opposite bank of the Nile is another great kingdom, stretching a distance of more than eight days' marching, the king of which has the title of Daw. The inhabitants of this region use arrows when fighting. Beyond this country lies another called Malal, the king of which is known as "The Muslim." He is thus called because his country became afflicted with drought one year following another; the inhabitants prayed for rain, sacrificing cattle until they had exterminated almost all of them, but the drought and the misery only increased. The king had as his guest a Muslim who used to read the Koran and was acquainted with the Sunna. To this man the king complained of the calamities that assailed him and his people. The man said: "O King, if you believed in God (who is exalted) and testified that He is One, and testified as to the prophetic mission of Muhammad (may God bless him and grant him peace) and if you accepted all the religious laws of Islam, I would pray for your deliverance from your plight and that God's mercy would envelop all the people of your country and that your enemies and adversaries might envy you on that account." Thus he continued to press the king until the latter accepted Islam and became a sincere Muslim. The man made him recite from the Koran some easy passages and taught him the religious obligations and practices which no one may be excused from knowing. Then the Muslim made him wait till the eve of the following Friday, when he ordered him to purify himself by a complete ablution, and clothed him in a cotton garment which he had. The two of them came out towards a mound of earth, and there the Muslim stood praying while the king, standing at his right side, imitated him. Thus they prayed for a part of the night, the Muslim reciting invocations and the king saying, "Amen." The dawn had just started to break when God caused abundant rain to descend upon them. So the king ordered the idols to be broken and expelled the sorcerers from his country. He and his descendants after him as well as his nobles were sincerely attached to Islam, while the common people of his kingdom remained polytheists. Since then their rulers have been given the title, "The Muslim."

Among the provinces of Ghana is a region called Sama, the inhabitants of which are known as the Bukm. From that region to Ghana is four days' travel. The people there go naked; only the women cover their sexual parts with strips of leather which they plait. They leave the hair on the pubis and only shave their heads. Abu 'Abd Allah al-Makki related that he saw one of these women stop in front of an Arab, who had a long beard, and say something that he could not understand. He asked the interpreter about the meaning of her words. He replied that she wished that she had hair like that of his beard on her pubis. The Arab, filled with anger, called down curses upon her.

The Bukm are very skillful archers and use poisoned arrows. Among them the eldest son inherits all the property of his father.

West from the town of Ghana is that of Anbara. Its king, named Tarim, is opposed to the ruler of Ghana. Nine stages from Anbara and fifteen from Ghana is the town of Kugha, the people of which are Muslims though the country around is inhabited by polytheists. Most of the goods imported there consist of salt, cowries, copper, and euphorbium. The latter commodity and cowries are the wares most in demand there. In the surrounding country are many gold mines. This region is the most productive in gold of all the land of the Sudan. There is also the town of

ʿLWKN, the king of which, Qanmar b. Basi by name, they say is a Muslim but conceals his religion.

In the country of Ghana live people called the Hunayhin who are descendants of the troops which the Banu Umayya sent to Ghana during the first epoch of Islam. They now follow the religion of the people of Ghana, but they do not take wives from among the Sudan, nor do they give their daughters in marriage to them. They are white of complexion, with handsome countenances. At Sila also there is a group of these people, called al-Faman.

The custom of trial by water exists in the land of Ghana. When a man is accused of denying a debt, or having shed blood, or some other crime, the official in charge takes a thin piece of wood, which is sour and bitter to taste, and pours upon it some water, which he then gives to the defendant to drink. If the man vomits his innocence is recognized, and he is congratulated. If he does not vomit and the drink remains in his stomach the accusation is accepted as justified . . . .

If from Ghana you direct yourself towards the sunrise you go along a road through country inhabited by Sudan to a place called Awgham. The people there cultivate sorghum which is their staple food. Then you go for four days to the place called *Ra's al-Ma'* ["head of the water"], and there you meet the Nile coming out of the land of the Sudan. Tribes of Muslim Berbers, called Madasa, inhabit one of its banks, and opposite them on the other bank live the pagan Sudan. Then you go from there six stages along the Nile to the town of Tiraqqa. In the market of that town the people of Ghana and Tadmekka assemble . . . .

From Tiraqqa the Nile turns towards the south into the land of the Sudan, and you go along it for about three stages, and then enter the country of the Saghmara, who are a Berber tribe living in the province of Tadmekka. On the opposite bank is the town of Kawkaw, which belongs to the Sudan. A description of this town and the neighboring ones will be given in another place, if God wills . . . .

From . . . Tiraqqa . . . across the desert plain [one goes to] to Tadmekka, which of all the towns of the world is the one that resembles Makka the most. Its name means "the Makka-like." It is a large town amidst mountains and ravines and is better built than Ghana or Kawkaw. The inhabitants of Tadmekka are Muslim Berbers who veil themselves as the Berbers of the desert do. They live on meat and milk as well as on a grain which the earth produces without being tilled. Sorghum and other grains are imported for them from the land of the Sudan. They wear clothes of cotton, *nuli*, and other robes dyed red. Their king wears a red turban, yellow shirt, and blue trousers. Their dinars are called "bald" because they are of pure gold without any stamp. Their women are of perfect beauty, unequaled among people of any other country, but adultery is allowed among them. They fall upon any merchant [disputing as to] which of them shall take him to her house . . .

When a traveler goes from the country of Kawkaw along the bank of the river in a westerly direction he reaches the kingdom called Damdam, the people of which eat anyone who falls into their hands. They have a great king to whom minor rulers are subject. In their country is a huge fortress surmounted by an idol in the form of a woman which they worship as their God and to which they go on pilgrimage.

Between Tadmekka and the town of Kawkaw is a distance of nine stages. The Arabs call the inhabitants of the latter town BZRKANYYN. This town consists of two towns, one being the residence of the king and the other inhabited by the Muslims. The king is called Qanda. The clothes of the people there are like those of the other Sudan, consisting of a robe and a garment of skins or some other material, according to each man's individual means. They worship idols as do the other Sudan. When their king sits down [to partake of a meal] a drum is beaten, and Sudanese women dance with their thick hair flowing, and nobody in the town goes about his business until he has finished his repast, the remnants of which are thrown into the Nile. At this [the courtiers] shout boisterously so that the people know that the king has finished his meal. When a king ascends the throne he is handed a signet ring, a sword, and a copy of the Koran which, as they assert, were sent to them by the Commander of the Faithful. Their king is a Muslim, for they entrust the kingship only to Muslims. They maintain that they are called Kawkaw because this word can be heard in the noise of their drums. In the same way the names of Azwar, Hir, and Zawila are heard in the drumbeats of these people, saying: "Zawila, Zawila." The people of the region of Kawkaw trade with salt which serves as their currency. This salt is obtained from an underground mine at Tutak, in Berber country, and transported to Tadmekka and thence to Kawkaw. Between Tadmekka and Tutak is a distance of six stages.

5. The Conversion of Ghana and Its Neighbors, the Struggle for Religious Conformity, Slave Raiding and Trading

AL-ZUHRI (c. 1130-1155)

Nothing is known about al-Zuhri; even his own name and that of his father are not the same in different manuscripts. From internal evidence we know that he visited towns in Spain between 1137 and 1154. The most accessible printed text, edited by Hadj Sadok, is not entirely satisfactory due to the great difficulties presented by the manuscripts. Al-Zuhri refers to the land of black people not by the Arab term bilad al-sudan, *but by the corresponding Berber term for black people,* Janawa; *other Arab writers also use variations of this term, such as Ganawa, Ginawa or Kinawa occasionally. Al-Zuhri gives a date for the conversion to Islam of the people of Ghana. In the printed text this date is 496/1102–3. The correct date, however, is 469/1076–77; this is the date in all other manuscripts of al-Zuhri, and also that of the fourteenth-century work entitled* al-Hulal al-Mawshiyya, *whose anonymous author had copied from a manuscript of al-Zuhri as early as 1381:*

> Abu ʿAbd Allah b. Yahya al-Zuhri *says that the people of the lands of the Sudan whose capital is the city of Ghana formerly professed Christianity until the year 469/1076–77 when they turned Muslim and became good Muslims. That was when the* amir *Abu Yahya son of the* amir *Abu Bakr b. ʿUmar al-Lamtuni made his appearance.*

Source: N. Levtzion and J.F.P. Hopkins, *Corpus of Early Arabic Sources for West African History* (Princeton: Markus Wiener Publishers, 2000 and 2006), pp. 94–99.

The conversion, according to al-Zuhri, occurred "when Yahya b. Abi Bakr the amir of Masufa made his appearance. They turned Muslims in the days of the Lamtuna." Yahya b. Abi Bakr b. ʿUmar was the leader of the Almoravids in the southern Sahara. The text of al-Hulal al-Mawshiyya *says that Abu Bakr was of the Lamtuna, not the Masufa as in al-Zuhri's text.*

Al-Zuhri associates the conversion of Ghana together with the conversion of Tadmekka and Zafun. Zafun will be referred to in greater detail by Yaqut (writing 1224). Al-Zuhri says that the people of Zafun had become Muslims long ago, but that they had adopted a school [of religious doctrine] that took them outside holy law. They returned to Orthodox Islam together with the people of Ghana and Tadmekka. However, Tadmekka, according to the same text of al-Zuhri, was converted only seven years after the conversion of Ghana. It was probably during these seven years, when Ghana was politically associated with the Almoravids, that Ghana sought the help of the Almoravids against Tadmekka. The Almoravids eradicated Ibadi communities from the southern Sahara (Awdaghust and Tadmekka) and from most of the oases of the northern Sahara.

Al-Zuhri considered Ghana the capital of the Janawa; they also included the tribe of Amima, who had no iron weapons and were therefore raided for slaves by the peoples of Ghana, who did have swords and spears. The pagan Barbara were raided for slaves, but at the same time were recognized for their nobility of blood because they were related to the king of Ghana.

The Third Section: Janawa

In it there is the town of Ghana. Between this town and the Great Sea to the west there is eight days' traveling. It is the capital of Janawa. Caravans from the land of the farthest Sus and the Maghrib go there. In former times the people of this country professed paganism until the year 469/1076–1077 when Yahya b. Abu Bakr the *amir* of Masufa made his appearance. They turned Muslim in the days of Lamtuna and became good Muslims. Today they are Muslims and have scholars, lawyers, and Koran readers and have become pre-eminent in these fields. Some of their chief leaders have come to al-Andalus [Islamic Spain]. They have traveled to Makka and made the Pilgrimage and visited the Prophet's tomb and returned to their land to spend large sums on the Holy War.

From this country desert slaves are imported. The people of Ghana make raids on the land of Barbara and Amima and capture their people as they used to do when they were pagans. Amima are a tribe of Janawa who live on the coast of the Great Sea in the west. They follow the religion of the Majus. On account of their paganism no one enters their country and no merchandise is imported into it. They wear sheep skins. They have plenty of honey and live in the sand without any building except tents which they make from desert grasses. The people of Ghana make raids on them every year. Sometimes they conquer them and sometimes they are conquered. These people have no iron and fight only with clubs of ebony. For this reason the people of Ghana overcome them, for they fight them with swords and spears. Any slave of them can run on his own legs faster than a thoroughbred horse.

Near to Ghana at a distance of fifteen days' traveling there are two towns, one of which is called NSLA and the second Tadmekka. Between these two towns is a distance of nine days' traveling. The people of these two towns turned Muslim seven years after the people of Ghana turned Muslim. There had been much warfare between them. The people of Ghana sought the help of the Almoravids. The people of Tadmekka make raids on the land of the Barbara, a tribe of Janawa. The Barbara, in their own opinion, are the most noble and aristocratic of men. This is because the amir of Ghana is related to them and used to be one of them. Every amir of the land of Janawa acknowledges their nobility except the

25

Muslims, since the highest nobility belongs to those who believe in God and His Prophet and the Last Day . . . .

About twenty *farsakhs* [leagues] to the east of Ghana is the town of Zafun. This is the nearest of the desert towns to Waraqlan and Sijilmasa. Between these two towns the Almoravids live. These people accepted Islam when the people of Waraqlan did so in the time of [the Umayyad Caliph] Hisham b. ʿAbd al-Malik [105/724–125/743]. But [then] they adopted a school [of religious doctrine] that took them outside the Holy Law. They returned to orthodox Islam when the people of Ghana, Tadmekka and Zafun adopted Islam. They are attached to the town of Ghana because it is their capital and the seat of their kingdom.

The people of Zafun take captives from the people of Amima, a tribe of the Janawa who live in the eastern part of the desert between Zafun and Kawkaw near the Nile of Egypt. They are people who profess Judaism. Their country is entered from Kawkaw and Waraqlan. They are the poorest of the Janawa. They read the Torah.

6. Twelfth-Century Peoples and Polities of the Sudanic Belt Surveyed from West (Takrur) to East (Nubia), Slave Raiding and Trading, Diverse African Customs

AL-IDRISI (1154)

Abu 'Abd Allah Muhammad al-Idrisi, a sharif *or descendant of the prophet, was probably Moroccan. Al-Idrisi was the best-known Arab geographer in Europe. His work, completed in 1154, was written at the request of Roger II, the Norman king of Sicily, and it is often referred to as the* Kitab Rujar *or "Book of Roger." Al-Idrisi's work was one of the first Arabic books ever to be printed; a press in Rome issued an abridgement as early as 1592.*

Al-Idrisi's great geographical work was designed as a companion to a map. The original large silver planisphere has not survived, but two dimensional written maps do accompany some of the extant manuscripts. Al-Idrisi adhered to the Ptolemaic tradition of geographical thinking, but often he did not successfully integrate the new empirical evidence accumulated since Ptolemy's day by the Arabs into the older, dominant conceptual framework. Wherever he failed, the inevitable result was a distortion of geographical and historical realities.

Al-Idrisi followed Ptolemy in assuming that all the southern lands lay in an arid torrid zone, where life depended completely on the river: "There is no rain at all in the town of Bilaq, nor in all the other regions of the Sudan . . . . They have no rain or mercy from God nor succor other than the inundation of the Nile, on which they rely for agriculture." Al-Idrisi described the route from Ghana to Mali as "being over dunes and

Source: N. Levtzion and J.F.P. Hopkins, *Corpus of Early Arabic Sources for West African History* (Princeton: Markus Wiener Publishers, 2000 and 2006), pp. 106–15, passim.

deep sands where there is no water." If their country was a desert, the people of Lamlam, who lived deeper in the interior of Africa, bred camels. These wrong assumptions led al-Idrisi to believe that in this part of the world no town could have existed away from the river. Therefore, al-Idrisi placed all the towns of the Sudan, including the capital of Ghana, on the banks of the Nile. Here as elsewhere in the Arab geographical literature the river conceptualized as the "Nile" combines imperfectly compre-hended information about a number of great African rivers into one great, meandering stream that was visualized as passing through the lands of the Sudan and Nubia.

Al-Idrisi consulted the text of al-Bakri as he wrote, and modified it according to his own geographical concepts. He also updated al-Bakri's information in regard to several details that might explain certain changes that took place after the Almoravids' adventures in the southern Sahara and the Sudan. For example, by the time of al-Idrisi Awdaghust had become a small town with little trade. Also the authority of Takrur seems to have spread up the Senegal River, because according to al-Idrisi, Barisa, close to the gold fields, paid tribute to the king of Takrur. This might have been because of Takrur's alliance with the Almoravids. According to al-Bakri, the son of the king of Takrur had joined the Almoravids in their battle against the Gudala.

Nevertheless, al-Idrisi's historical facts must be read very critically, such as his assertion that in the twelfth century towns close to the coun-try of gold were still "subject to the ruler of Ghana, to whom they pay their taxes." According to al-Idrisi Ghana was still a powerful kingdom. Its monarch was a Muslim, but we doubt al-Idrisi's claim that this king was a sharif by descent.

Al-Idrisi identified four ethnographical regions in bilad al-Sudan: *the land of Lamlam is that of primitive little-known peoples whose neighbors raid them. No one lives to the south of the Lamlam. To their north is Ghana (the Soninke ethnic group), to their west is the land of the*

Maqzara (the land of the Wolof and the Tokolor, who speak languages of the West Atlantic family), and to their east the land of Wangara or Wanqara. Al-Idrisi used the term Wangara to refer both to the land where gold originated and to the people who spoke Mandingue, particularly those who were traders. Thus al-Idrisi could refer to Tiraqqa as "one of the towns of Wangara" because it was a market where "the people of Ghana and Tadmekka assemble," and despite the fact, recorded by al-Bakri, that it lay far from the land of gold.

The First Clime

. . . All the other lands in the neighborhood of the Nile are empty waste, where there is no settlement. In these wastes there are arid waterless deserts, where water can only be found after two, four, five, six, or twelve days' [marching], as in the arid desert of Nisar, which is on the route from Sijilmasa to Ghana . . . . In the land of the Sudan there are many arid deserts like this. Most of its terrain is sand that is swept by the winds, and carried from place to place, and no water is found there. This land is very hot and scorching. Because of the intensity of the heat and the burning sun, the inhabitants of this First Clime as well as those of the Second and part of the Third Climes are black in color, with crinkled hair, in contrast with the complexion of the people of the Sixth and Seventh Climes . . . . .

Sila belongs to the domains of the Takruri, who is a powerful ruler. He has slaves and soldiers, strength and firmness as well as widely-known justice. His country is safe and calm. His place of residence and his capital is the town of Takrur, on the south bank of the Nile. Between that town and Sila is a distance of about two days' traveling by the river or by land. The town of Takrur is larger than Sila, and has more trade. The people of Morocco go there with wool, copper and beads, and they export from there gold and slaves . . . . .

29

From the town of Takrur to that of Barisa, which is on the Nile, going to the east is twelve stages. The town of Barisa is a small town that has no wall, but is like a populous village. Its inhabitants are itinerant merchants who pay allegiance to the Takruri.

South of Barisa, at a distance of about ten days, is the land of Lamlam. The people of Barisa, Sila and Ghana make forays into the land of Lamlam and capture its inhabitants. They bring them to their own countries and sell them to the visiting merchants. The latter export them to all the countries. In the whole land of Lamlam there are only two small village-like towns, one called Malal and the other Daw. Between these two towns is a distance of about four days. Their inhabitants, according to the reports of the people of that part of the world, are Jews, [but] infidelity and ignorance overcame them. When, among all the people of Lamlam, one reaches puberty, he is branded on his face and temples with fire, and this is their mark. Their country and all their settlements are in a river valley, which joins the Nile.

Beyond the land of Lamlam to the south there is no known habitation. The country of Lamlam adjoins, in the west, that of Maqzara, in the east the land of Wangara, in the north the land of Ghana, and in the south the uninhabited lands. Their speech does not resemble that of the people of Maqzara, or that of the people of Ghana.

From the afore-mentioned Barisa to Ghana takes twelve days in an easterly direction. Barisa is halfway [from Ghana] to the towns of Sila and Takrur. Likewise from the town of Barisa to Awdaghust is twelve stages. Awdaghust is north of Barisa . . . .

The weapons of the people of this country are bows and arrows, on which they mostly rely, but they also use maces which they make of ebony with much cunning and craft. Their bows are made of the *sharki* reed. The arrows and bow-strings, too, are of reed.

The people of this land build their houses of mud, because wide and long pieces of wood are scarce there.

Their adornments are of copper, little beads, strings of glass [beads], and [the stones called] *badhuq* and "old man's slobber," and various kinds of false onyx manufactured from glass. All these facts and circumstances that we have mentioned concerning their foodstuffs, drinks, clothing and ornaments, are common to the majority of the Sudan throughout their land, for it is a fiercely hot country. The townsmen in that country culti- vate onions, gourds and watermelons, which grow very large there, but they have no wheat nor any grain other than sorghum, from which they make an intoxicating drink. The bulk of their meat comes from fish and camel-meat cut into strips and dried in the sun, as we have already described . . . .

The Second Section of the First Clime

Among the towns in this section are Malal, Ghana, Tiraqqa, Madasa, Saghmara, Ghiyara, Gharbil and Samaqanda. We have already mentioned the town of Malal, which is in the country of Lamlam. It is a small town, like a large village without a surrounding wall, built on an unassailable hill of red earth. The people of Malal seek protection there from the other Sudan, who attack them. They drink from a running spring which issues from the mountain that stands south of the town. Its water is brackish, not truly sweet.

West of that town, by the spring from which they drink, and along its course as far as its confluence with the Nile, live numerous peoples of the Sudan, who are naked and do not cover themselves with anything at all. They marry without paying any dower or bride-price. Of all people they are the most prolific. They have camels and goats, on whose milk they live. They eat the fish which they catch and sun-dried camel meat. Peoples of the neighboring countries continually capture them, using var- ious tricks. They take them away to their own lands, and sell them in droves to the merchants. Every year great numbers of them are sent to

Morocco. Everyone in the land of Lamlam is branded on the face with fire, which is their mark, as we have mentioned before.

From the town of Malal to the town of Great Ghana is about twelve stages over dunes and deep sands where there is no water. Ghana consists of two towns on both banks of the river. This is the greatest of all the towns of the Sudan in respect of area, the most populous, and with the most extensive trade. Prosperous merchants go there from all the surrounding countries and the other lands of the extreme west. Its people are Muslims, and its king, according to what is reported, belongs to the progeny of Salih son of ʿAbd Allah son of Hasan son of al-Hasan son of ʿAli b. Abu Talib. The sermon at the Friday communal prayers is delivered in his own name, though he pays allegiance to the ʿAbbasid caliph. He has a palace on the bank of the Nile, strongly built and perfectly fortified. His living quarters are decorated with various drawings and paintings, and provided with glass windows. This palace was built in the year 510 of the Hijra [1116–17 C.E.].

His kingdom and his land adjoin the land of Wangara. This is the country of gold, which is [often] mentioned and described as having quantities of it of good quality. The people of Morocco know positively and without difference of opinion that the king has in his palace a brick of gold weighing thirty pounds made of one piece. It is entirely God's creation, without having been melted in the fire or hammered with any tool. A hole has been pierced in it to serve for tethering the king's horse. It is one of those curious objects that no one else possesses and which is not permissible for anyone else. He prides himself on it above the other kings of the Sudan. According to what is related about him, he is the most righteous of men. One of his practices in keeping close to the people and upholding justice among them is that he has a corps of army commanders who come on horseback to his palace every morning. Each commander has a drum, which is beaten before him. When he reaches the gate it is silenced. When all the commanders have assembled, the king mounts

32

his horse and rides at their head through the lanes of the town and around it. Anyone who has suffered injustice or misfortune confronts him, and stays there until the wrong is remedied. Then he returns to his palace, and the commanders disperse. Following the afternoon prayer, when the heat of the sun abates, he mounts his horse again and comes out, surrounded by his soldiers, but [this time] no one may approach him or reach him. His riding, twice every day, is a well-known practice and this is what is famous about his justice.

His garments consist of a silk cloth that he wraps around himself or a mantle in which he envelops himself; loose trousers cover the middle of his body, and he wears sandals made of *sharki* [reed] on his feet. His mounts are horses. He has handsome ornaments and excellent attire, which are carried in front of him on his feast days. He has many flags and one banner. Ahead of him go elephants, giraffes and other kinds of wild animals, which are found in the country of the Sudan.

The people of Ghana have strongly made boats on the Nile, which they use for fishing or for moving about between the two towns. The clothing of these people consists of waist-wrappers, loincloths, and mantles, everyone dressing himself according to his pretensions.

To the west the land of Ghana adjoins the country of Maqzara; to the east, the country of Wangara; to the north, the desert that extends between the land of the Sudan and the land of the Berbers; and to the south it adjoins the land of the Lamlam and other infidels.

From the town of Ghana to the beginning of the country of Wangara is eight days' journey. This country of Wangara is the country of the gold, famous on account of its good quality and abundance. It is an island 300 miles long and 150 miles wide, surrounded by the Nile on all sides during the whole year. In the month of August, when the heat becomes intense, and the Nile leaves its bed and overflows, it covers this island, or most of it. It remains thus for its regular period and then starts to recede. When it begins to recede and go down, all those in the country of the

Sudan return, flocking to that island in search [of gold]. They search as long as the Nile is receding, each one finding there what God, praise be unto him, allows, whether a large or a small quantity of gold, none being completely disappointed. When the Nile has returned to its [upper] level, these people sell whatever gold has fallen into their hands, trading with each other. The people of Warqalan and Morocco buy most of the gold and export it to the mints in their own country, where dinars are struck from it, which they use in trade. Thus it happens every year, and this is the greatest source of income for the Sudan, upon which both great and small rely.

In the land of Wangara there are flourishing towns and famous strongholds. Its inhabitants are rich, for they possess gold in abundance, and many good things are imported to them from the outermost parts of the earth. Their clothing consists of waist-wrappers, mantles, and chemises.

Tiraqqa is one of the towns of Wangara. It is a large town, inhabited by many people, but it has no surrounding wall nor enclosure. Tiraqqa is subject to the ruler of Ghana, in whose name the sermon at the Friday communal prayers is delivered, and to whom the people go in litigation. The road from Ghana to Tiraqqa is along the Nile, a distance of six days' [journey] . . . .

West of Gharbil at [a distance of] eleven stages is the town of Ghiyara, which is on the bank of the Nile, and is surrounded by a moat. There are many people there, who are renowned for their courage and wisdom. They make raids on the land of the Lamlam, capture them, bring them back and sell them to the merchants of Ghana. Between Ghiyara and the land of Lamlam is thirteen stages. [The people of Ghiyara] ride thoroughbred camels. Taking with them provisions of water, they travel by night, and reach the land of Lamlam in the daytime. [As soon as] they succeed in capturing their booty, they return to their country with the captives they have succeeded in taking from the people of Lamlam. From the town of Ghiyara to that of Ghana is eleven stages. There is little water in Ghiyara. All the lands we have described are subject to the ruler of Ghana, to whom people pay their taxes, and he is their protector . . . .

The Third Section of the First Clime

The town of Kawkaw is large and is widely famed in the land of the Sudan. It is on the bank of a river, which flows from the north, and passes by the town. Its people drink from it. Many of the Sudan say that the town of Kawkaw is on the bank of the [sic] canal while others say that it is on a river which flows into the Nile. The right opinion is, that this river flows on till it is many days past Kawkaw, and then loses itself in the waste in the dunes and quicksands as does the river Euphrates in Iraq, which disappears into the marshes.

The king of the town of Kawkaw is an independent ruler, who has the sermon at the Friday communal prayers delivered in his own name. He has many servants and a large retinue, captains, soldiers, excellent apparel and beautiful ornaments. [His warriors] ride horses and camels; they are brave and superior in might to all the nations who are their neighbors around their land. The clothing of the common people of Kawkaw consists of skins with which they cover their nudity. Their merchants wear chemises and mantles, and woolen bands rolled around their heads. Their ornaments are of gold. The nobles and eminent persons among them wear waist-wrappers. They mix with the merchants, sit in their company, and take shares in their wares [participating in the profit] by way of *commenda* contracts . . . .

There are twelve stages from Tamalma to the town of Manan in the land of Kanim. Manan is a small town without industry of any sort and little commerce. Its people breed camels and goats.

From the town of Manan to that of Anjimi is eight days' [traveling]. The latter is also in Kanim. Anjimi is a very small town, and has but few inhabitants of the humblest kind. To the east, they are neighbors of the Nuba. Between the town of Anjimi and the Nile is three days' [traveling] in a southerly direction. Its people drink [water] from wells.

From Anjimi to the town of Zaghawa is six days' [traveling]. The town of Zaghawa is well populated and is the center for several districts. Around it live many of the Zaghawa, who carry goods with their camels. They have a little trade and manufacture objects with which they trade among themselves. They drink water from wells, and eat sorghum, sun-dried camel meat, and the fish they catch; they also have abundant milk. Their clothing consists of dyed skins with which they cover themselves. They are the scabbiest of all the Sudan.

From the town of Zaghawa to Manan is eight stages. In Manan live the ruler and governor [of the country]. Most of his men are naked archers who shoot with bows.

From the town of Manan to the town of Tajuwa is thirteen stages. This is the capital of the Tajuwa people, who are pagans, and do not believe in anything. Their land adjoins that of the Nuba. Another town in their country is Samna, which is a small town. A traveler who had been to the country of Kawar related that the ruler of Bilaq, who is a governor on behalf of the king of the Nuba, turned against Samna, and burned and destroyed it, scattering its inhabitants in all directions. It is now in ruins. Samna is six stages distant from the town of Tajuwa. There are eighteen stages from the town of Tajuwa to that of Nuwabiya, from which the Nuba trace their origin, and derive their name . . . .

The Fourth Section of the First Clime

There is no rain at all in the town of Bilaq [in the land of the Nuba], or in all the other regions of the Sudan, such as the Nuba, the Habasha, and the people of Kanim, the Zaghawa, and other nations. They have no rains, nor mercy from God, nor succor other than the inundation of the Nile, on which they rely for agriculture.

36

7. Kings, Merchants, and Policing the Trade across the Western Sahara in Almohad Times

AL-SARAKHSI (1197-1203)

Taj al-Din b. Hamawayh al-Sarakhsi came to the Maghrib from the east, and served at the court of the Almohads in Marrakech between 1197 and 1203. Only a few fragments of his work survived, as quotations in a work entitled Nafh al-Tib *by al-Maqqari (1591–1632 C.E.) Al-Sarakhsi's brief paragraph illustrates the importance of the trade across the Sahara. The Almohad governor of Sijilmasa, a gateway to the Sahara, beheaded those who robbed travelers on the route to Ghana. The same governor, who died in 1203 C.E., sent a letter to "the king of the Sudan in Ghana," who detained traders from the Maghrib. "We are neighbors in benevolence," he wrote, "even if we differ in religion." This non-Muslim king of the Sudan in Ghana was in all probability the king of Soso, who had conquered Ghana, and who according to oral traditions persecuted Muslim traders. One may therefore infer that the Soso had conquered Ghana by about 1200 C.E.*

He [al-Sarakhsi] says in his *Rihla* when mentioning the *sayyid* Abu'l-Rabiʿ Sulayman b. ʿAbd Allah, son of the Commander of the Faithful ʿAbd al-Muʾmin b. ʿAli, who was at that time governor of Sijilmasa and its districts: "I met him when he came to Marrakech after the death of al-Mansur Yaʿqub to take the oath of allegiance to his son Muhammad. I found him to be an old man of striking appearance and excellent charac-

Source: N. Levtzion and J.F.P. Hopkins, *Corpus of Early Arabic Sources for West African History* (Princeton: Markus Wiener Publishers, 2000 and 2006), p. 372.

ter, eloquent in Arabic and Berber. These are some of his words in a letter of reply to the king of the Sudan in Ghana, complaining to him of the
detention of some traders: 'We are neighbors in benevolence even if we
differ in religion; we agree on right conduct and are one in leniency
towards our subjects. It goes without saying that justice is an essential
quality of kings in conducting sound policy; tyranny is the preoccupation
of ignorant and evil minds. We have heard about the imprisonment of
poor traders and their being prevented from going freely about their business. The coming to and fro of merchants to a country is of benefit to its
inhabitants and a help to keeping it populous. If we wished we would
imprison the people of that region who happen to be in our territory but
we do not think it right to do that. We ought not to "forbid immorality
while practicing it ourselves." Peace be upon you.'

"The holy man Abu ʿAbd Allah Muhammad al-Qastallani said to me:
'I went into the presence of Abu'l-Rabiʿ in the palace of Sijilmasa. He had
before him leather mats upon which were the heads of the rebels who had
robbed travelers on the highway between Sijilmasa and Ghana . . .' He
[Abu'l-Rabiʿ] died after the year 600/1203–4."

Yaqut b. ʿAbd Allah al-Hamawi al-Rumi, as the final part of his name indicates, was a Greek (Rumi) by origin. Born in 1179, he was captured in Byzantine territory and then sold to a Syrian merchant who lived in Baghdad. Yaqut's master gave him a good education, and later sent him to trade on his behalf; he freed him in 1199. Yaqut then continued to travel widely in the provinces of Iran, Iraq, Syria and Egypt. Books were his main concern, and for some time he earned his living by copying books and selling them. He explored libraries in almost every major town he visited. A tireless compiler and encyclopedist, Yaqut wrote his geographical dictionary between 1212 and 1229. He arranged place names in alphabetical order. He regularly named his sources, which belong to very different periods, such as the now-lost work of the tenth-century writer al-Muhallabi. The text quoted by Yaqut from al-Muhallabi appeas as a separate text (no. 3) in the present volume.

Yaqut's only original contribution concerns Zafun, a previously poorly-known kingdom on the margins of the Sahara. Before Yaqut, Zafun had been mentioned by al-Zuhri and by an anonymous work entitled Kitab al-istibsar, *written about 1135 and updated in 1191. The people of Zafun, according to the latter source, were Berbers. Yaqut's description of the king of Zafun, who was both very black and veiled, combines traits to be expected of Sudan and Berbers. It is probable that Yaqut's account of*

Source: N. Levtzion and J.F.P. Hopkins, *Corpus of Early Arabic Sources for West African History* (Princeton: Markus Wiener Publishers, 2000 and 2006), pp. 170-71.

Zafun properly belongs to the second quarter of the twelfth century, when the power of the Almoravids had declined to such an extent that the Almoravid ruler might have shown such great deference to the king of Zafun.

Yaqut's information thus belongs to the age of transition between the realm of the Almoravids and the rise of the empire of Mali. Both oral traditions collected recently and the seventeenth-century West African Arabic history, the Tarikh al-Fattash, *contribute additional information about this dimly-seen period; however, they use a different nomenclature that requires explanation. It is likely that Zafun may be identified with Diafunu, which the* Tarikh al-Fattash *described thus: "There was an ancient and important town, which was built before Diara, and preceded it as a capital. It was the town of the people of Diafunu, who are known as Diafunke. It existed in the time of the Kaya-Magha, and was destroyed when the kingdom of the Kaya-Magha collapsed as a result of their wars. Diara was founded after its destruction." Oral traditions make the Kaya-Magha the ruler of Wagadu, the ancient Soninke state, which is probably the same land as the "Ghana" of the external Arabic sources.*

Zafun [spelled out] is a vast province in the land of the Sudan, near the Maghrib, and adjoining the land of the veiled people. The people of Zafun have a powerful and redoubtable king. He has a capital, which they call Zafun. He leads a nomadic life, seeking [pasture] in places where the rains have fallen. This used to be the way of life of the veiled people before they took possession of the Maghrib. The king of Zafun is stronger than the latter and more versed in the art of kingship. The veiled people acknowledge his superiority over them, obey him and resort to him in all important matters of government. One year this king, on his way to the Pilgrimage, came to the Maghrib to pay a visit to the Commander of the Muslims, the veiled king of the Maghrib, of the tribe of the Lamtuna. The Commander of the Muslims met him on foot, whereas the [king of] Zafun did not dismount for him. A certain person who saw him in Marrakech on the day he came there said that he was tall, of deep black complexion and veiled. The whites of his eyes were bloodshot as if they were two glowing coals, and the palms of his hands were yellow as if tinted with saffron. He was wearing a cut garment enveloped in a white cloak. He entered the palace of the Commander of the Muslims mounted, while the latter walked in front of him.

9. Thirteenth-Century Peoples and Polities of the Sudanic Belt Surveyed from West (Canary Islands) to East (Nubia), with an Emphasis on Kanim

IBN SA'ID (1269-1287)

'Ali b. Musa Ibn Sa'id was born in Granada in 1214 and died in Tunis in 1286–87. His geographical work was written some time after 1269. He was concerned with the exact location of places according to their coordinates of latitude and longitude. Like al-Idrisi, he divided the earth into seven climes, and then each clime into sections.

Ibn Sa'id made the important observation that the people of Maqzara (Takrur) were divided between some who were sedentary and others who were nomads. This is probably the earliest reference to the pastoral Fulbe, who speak the same language as do the sedentary Tokolor of Takrur. Ibn Sa'id recorded the accounts of the traveler Ibn Fatima, particularly on Lake Chad (which he calls "Lake Kuri") and on Kanim, which had been poorly represented by earlier geographers. According to Ibn Sa'id, the king of Kanim had converted four generations before his time, which suggests a date of about 1100; this is consistent with the statement of the anonymous author of the Kitab al-istibsar *(see Levtzion and Hopkins,* Corpus, *p. 138), that the people of Kanim embraced Islam some time after 500/1106–7.*

The king of Kanim, according to Ibn Sa'id, was of the posterity of Sayf son of Dhi Yazan, a pre-Islamic (sixth-century) Yemenite king who became a folk hero in Arab popular literature. This ancestry is mentioned again in the fourteenth century by al-Qalqashandi and al-Maqrizi (see below).

Source: N. Levtzion and J.F.P. Hopkins, *Corpus of Early Arabic Sources for West African History* (Princeton: Markus Wiener Publishers, 2000 and 2006), pp. 182–93.

According to Ibn Sa'id, the authority of the sultan of Kanim extended over Kawar and Fazzan, and the Berbers were slaves of the king of Kanim. He confirmed that during periods of strength Kanim expanded northward into the Sahara, rather than southward.

The First Section of the First Clime

Ibn Fatima relates: The Fortunate Isles, between the Canary Islands and the mainland, are scattered over the First, Second, and Third Climes. They consist of 24 islands and accounts of them resemble legends.

The Atlantic Ocean rises little by little in this section as far as the mouth of the Nile, which flows past Ghana and Takrur, where the longitude is 10° 20' and the latitude 14°. Facing the mouth of the Nile in the Atlantic Ocean at a distance of 1-1/2° is Salt Island. Its length from north to south is a little over 2° and its width 1/2°. On the coast of its southern extremity is the town of Awlil . . . . Its people live on fish and turtles and their trade is in salt. They carry it by ship up to the countries on the banks of the Nile. He [al-Idrisi] says: there is no other supply of salt in the land of the Sudan . . . .

[The people of Takrur] belong to a race called Mafzara or Maghzawa [people of Maqzara] and are divided into two sections: a section who are sedentary and live in towns, and a section who are nomads in the open country . . . .

The Third Section of the First Clime

Ibn Fatima says: "I have never met anyone who has seen [the] southern side [of Lake Chad]. It is navigated only by the Kanimis and their neighbors such as we encountered on the northern side. It is surrounded on all sides by peoples of the Sudan, cruel pagans who eat men. The best known of them are those whom we mention, [namely] the dwellers on the

43

north side, among whom are the Badi, after whom their city is named and from beneath which issues the Ghana Nile. Their territory is all round it. Their neighbors on the west are the Jabi or Jati. It is they who file their teeth. If there is a death among them they hand over the corpse to their neighbors for them to eat, and their neighbors do the same for them." To the south of the lake are the Inkizar and to the east the Kuri after whom it is named.

To the east of the town of Badi, among the Muslim Kanim, is Jaja. It is the seat of a separate kingdom with towns and villages now belonging to the sultan of Kanim. Fertility and abundance of the good things of life characterize it. There are peacocks there, and parrots, and speckled chickens, and piebald sheep of the size of small donkeys but shaped differently from our sheep. There are many giraffes in the land of Jaja. To the east of the town at the angle of the lake is al-Maghza where the sultan of Kanim's arsenal is situated. He often makes raids from there with his fleet on the lands of the pagans on the shores of this lake and attacks their ships and kills and takes prisoners. The city of Jaja is in longitude 48° 20', latitude 7°.

Level with the angle of the lake, where the longitude is 51°, there is one of the celebrated cities of Kanim called Manan. Its latitude is 13°. Southeast of it is Jimi, the capital of Kanim, where the longitude is 53° and the latitude 9°. There resides the sultan of Kanim, well known for his religious warfare and charitable acts, Muhammadi of the posterity of Sayf b. Dhi Yazan. The capital of his pagan ancestors before they adopted Islam was the town of Manan. A scholar converted his great-great-great-grandfather to Islam, and then Islam spread through the rest of the land of Kanim. This sultan has authority there over kingdoms such as those of the Tajuwa, Kawar, and Fazzan. God has assisted him and he has many descendants and armies. His clothes are brought to him from the capital of Tunis. He has scholars around him . . . .

The region where the Zaghawa wander is to the east of Manan. They are for the most part Muslims owing obedience to the sultan of Kanim. To the north of Manan and the territory of the Kanim the Akawwar wander. Their well-known towns are in the Second Clime and they are Muslims owing obedience to the sultan of Kanim.

The Fourth Section of the First Clime

Between the southeast [limit of the bend] of the Nile and Tajuwa, the capital of Zaghawa, there remains [no more than] 100 miles. This town is situated in longitude 55°, latitude 14°. Its people have adopted Islam and accepted the suzerainty of the sultan of Kanim. South of Tajuwa is the town of Zaghawa where the longitude is 54° and the latitude 11° 30'. The territory of the peoples of Tajuwa and Zaghawa extends over the tract lying within the bend of the Nile from south to north. They are of one race but authority and physical and moral excellence is found only among the people of Tajuwa. They are pagans who are refractory to the sultan of Kanim. They keep to the deserts and mountains of the First and Second Climes. Ibn Fatima relates that the kings of Kanim and Tajuwa fled with their capitals from the Nile only because of the mosquitoes which are abundant near the Nile and are very harmful to man and horses. They have wells in the sands and water that overflows from the Nile in periods of flood . . . .

The Second Section of the Second Clime

There is no town worthy of mention in this section except for Awdaghust. A mixture of Muslim Berbers inhabits it, but authority rests with the Sanhaja. There is an account of this town and its ruler in al-Bakri. It is on the line of the Second Clime in longitude 22°. In the same latitude is Zafun, which belongs to pagan Sudan and whose ruler enjoys a good reputation among the [other] kings of the Sudan.

The Third Section of the Second Clime

According to Ibn Fatima the first part of this section is like the preceding one in being under the sway of the desert, all shifting sands and no water . . . then [there is found] the land of the Kawar who are Muslim Sudan, and whose capital is called Kawar too. At present it is subject to the sultan of Kanim . . . . There is often strife over these two lakes between the inhabitants of Kawar, the Berbers of the desert, and the Arabs of Fazzan, for these factions are continually grazing their flocks on their shores . . . . The big mountain range of Luniya stretches from a point south of these cities to a point near the bend of the Egyptian Nile . . . .

To the north of this range, which stretches from west to east, is the country of the Barkami [or Tarkami] who are prosperous Sudan possessing valleys between the hills with palm trees, water, and verdure. Those of them who are adjacent to the country of the Kanim are Muslims, those who are adjacent to the country of the Nuba are Christians, and those who are adjacent to the country of the Zaghawa are idolators . . . . To the south of the Luniya mountains is the territory of the pagan Zaghawa, also known as the Shanwa or Sha'wa.

10. The Maqqari Brothers (c. 1250) Partnership Conducts Caravan Trade between the Mediterranean and Mali

IBN AL-KHATIB (1356)

The following account was recorded by Lisan al-Din Ibn al-Khatib (1313–75) in his native Granada. In 1356 a certain Muhammad al-Maqqari visited Granada. He presented himself as the great-grandson of Abu Bakr al-Maqqari, one of five brothers who operated a sophisticated commercial enterprise. This operation extended from Tlemcen near the Mediterranean to Sijilmasa, the gateway to the Sahara, and as far as Walata in the southern Sahara. The aforementioned Abu Bakr was the grandson of ʿAbd al-Rahman, a disciple of the great Sufi shaykh Abu Madyan, who died in 1197. By calculating four generations back from 1356 and three generations forward from 1197, the aforementioned Abu Bakr, and the operation of the Maqqari brothers, may be dated to the middle of the thirteenth century.

Takrur was first mentioned by al-Bakri as the name of a kingdom on the lower Senegal that became completely converted to Islam. By the thirteenth century the term had acquired a more general meaning; as Ibn Khallikan, who wrote between 1256 and 1274, put it, "Takrur is the name of the land where the Sudan live, and their race is called by the name of their land" (Levtzion and Hopkins, Corpus, *p. 164). During the hegemony of Mali, the Egyptians knew its ruler as "the king of Takrur" (see al-ʿUmari below). Therefore the conquest of Walata by Takrur refers here to the northward expansion of Mali and its annexation of Walata at the mid-*

Source: N. Levtzion and J.F.P. Hopkins, *Corpus of Early Arabic Sources for West African History* (Princeton: Markus Wiener Publishers, 2000 and 2006), pp. 307–8.

dle of the thirteenth century. The victorious king of Mali encouraged the Maqqari brothers to continue their trade, and cultivated relations with the rulers of the Maghrib.

[The words of] "Muhammad b. Muhammad b. Ahmad b. Abu Bakr . . . b. ʿAli al-Qurashi al-Maqqari, whose name of honor (*kunya*) is Abu ʿAbd Allah, judge of the community of Fez, a native of Tlemcen. I copied down from his own handwriting: "The one of our ancestors who adopted it [Tlemcen] as a place of settlement, it having been for his predecessors a place of visitation, was ʿAbd al-Rahman b. Abi Bakr b. ʿAli al-Maqqari the associate of Shaykh Abu Madyan, who offered to God for him and his posterity prayers of which the acceptance became manifest in them. He was my great-great-great-great grandfather, for I am Muhammad b. Muhammad b. Ahmad b. Abi Bakr b. Yahya b. ʿAbd al-Rahman. This holy man [Shaykh ʿAbd al-Rahman] was so assiduous in prayer that sometimes he would be put to the test in more than one way yet would not be perceived to turn round nor observed to show any awareness. It is said that this absorption was one of the things that he had learned at the sessions of his own spiritual master Shaykh Abu Madyan.

"Then his descendants, according to what is stated in their biographies, became famous in trade. They established the desert route by digging wells and seeing to the security of merchants. They introduced the drum as a starting signal and the standard that was carried in front while the caravan was on the move. The sons of Yahya, of whom Abu Bakr [my forefather] was one, were five. They made a partnership by which all had equal shares in what they possessed or might possess. Abu Bakr and Muhammad, who were the root-stocks of my pedigree on both my mother's and my father's side, were [near the Mediterranean] in Tlemcen; ʿAbd al-Rahman, who was their elder brother, was [at the Saharan oasis] in Sijilmasa; ʿAbd al-Wahid and ʿAli, who were their two younger brothers, were in Iwalatan [Walata, at the southern shore of the Sahara near the

Mali frontier]. They acquired properties and houses in those regions, married wives, and begat children by concubines. The Tilimsani [the brother at Tlemcen] would send to the Sahrawi [the brother at Walata] the goods that the latter would indicate to him, and the Sahrawi would send [back] to him skins, ivory, nuts, and gold. The Sijilmasi was like the tongue of a balance, indicating to them the extent of the rise or fall in the markets and writing to them about the affairs of merchants and countries. And so their wealth expanded and their status grew.

"When Takrur [Mali] conquered the region of Iwalatan [Walata] and its dependencies their wealth, along with the wealth of the region, was affected, although he [the Maqqari brother who was there] had gathered men together in defense of [the town and] his property. Then he entered into relations with their king, who made him welcome and enabled him to trade in all his country, addressing him as a dear and sincere friend. Then the king began to correspond with those [members of the Maqqari family] in Tlemcen, seeking from them the accomplishment of his desires and addressing him [them] in similar terms. I have letters from him and from the kings of the Maghrib that tell of this. When they had obtained the confidence of the kings the earth became submissive to their traveling upon it. Their wealth knew no bounds and became more than could be counted, for before the people of Egypt penetrated the desert lands there used to be imported to them from the Maghrib goods of inconsiderable value which were exchanged [in Mali] for a considerable price."

11. Kanim and Especially Mali According to Escorts of the Pilgrim King, *Mansa* Musa (1324)

AL-ʿUMARI (1336)

Ibn Fadl Allah al-ʿUmari was born in 1301 in Damascus and died there in 1349. He spent many years in Cairo, as an official in the administration of the Mamluk Sultanate. Al-ʿUmari wrote during the reign of Mansa Sulayman, shortly after Mansa Musa's death, because he says that the low price of the gold, caused by the pilgrimage of Mansa Musa in 1324, persisted for twelve years to the day of writing. Al-ʿUmari missed Mansa Musa's visit to Cairo because he was in Damascus at the time. But on his return to Cairo, he collected valuable information from Egyptian officials who had met Mansa Musa. Among his informants was also Abu ʿUthman Saʿid al-Dukkali, a Moroccan shaykh, who had lived for thirty-five years in the capital of Mali. According to al-ʿUmari several Berber chiefs recognized the authority of the king of Mali, whereas others were independent. Ibn Khaldun confirms that at certain periods the authority of the king of Mali was recognized far into the desert.

Whereas according to Ibn Saʿid and al-Maqrizi the first Muslim king of Kanim was of the Saifawa dynasty, al-ʿUmari suggests that there was a change of dynasty to the Saifawa after the conversion of Kanim. Al-ʿUmari updated Ibn Saʿid concerning Kanim from information by a certain Abu ʿAbd Allah al-Salaliji. According to al-ʿUmari, the people of Kanim were rigid in their religion, and had their own school in Cairo. Still, traits of divine kingship persisted, and even the king's ministers

Source: N. Levtzion and J.F.P. Hopkins, *Corpus of Early Arabic Sources for West African History* (Princeton: Markus Wiener Publishers, 2000 and 2006), pp. 259–74, passim.

spoke to him behind a curtain. His people saw him only at the two festi-
vals of Islam. Al-ʿUmari considered the king's behavior to be motivated
by arrogance. It is more likely, however, that the monarch acted as he did
out of weakness, for it was an age of internal discord in Kanim that even-
tually led to the dislocation of the seat of the kingdom to Borno. This was
the period of transition, because in al-ʿUmari's manual for scribes in the
Mamluk chancellery there are separate references to the ruler of Kanim
and to the ruler of Borno.

Chapter Nine:
The kingdoms of the Muslim Sudan on the bank of the Nile

Section 1—Kanim

The king of Kanim is an independent Muslim. Between him and the land
of Mali is a very long distance. The seat of his authority is a town called
Jimi. The beginning of his kingdom on the Egyptian side is a town called
Zala and its limit in longitude is a town called Kaka. There is a distance
between them of about three months' traveling. Their soldiers wear the
mouth-muffler. Their king, despite the feebleness of his authority and the
poverty of his soil, shows an inconceivable arrogance; despite the weakness of his troops and the small resources of his country, he touches with
his banner the clouds in the sky. He is veiled from his people. None sees
him save at the two festivals, when he is seen at dawn and in the afternoon. During the rest of the year nobody, not even the commander-in-
chief, speaks to him, except from behind a screen.

It happens sometimes that one of them gets a taste for instruction and
looks upon learning as he would the stars. He says: "I am ill" and keeps
treating his sick understanding and humoring his recalcitrant knowledge
until their rays shine upon him and he embroiders their advantages on his
brocade.

They live mostly on rice, wheat, and sorghum. There are figs, lemons, grapes, aubergines, and dates in their country. [Abu] ʿAbd Allah al-Salaliji informed me that he was told by the virtuous and ascetic shaykh ʿUthman al-Kanimi, who is related to their kings, that rice grows in their country without any seed whatever; and he was a reliable informant. Al-Salaliji stated that he asked others about the truth of this, and they said that it was true.

Their currency is a cloth that they weave, called *dandi*. Every piece is ten cubits long. They make purchases with it from a quarter of a cubit upwards. They also use cowries, beads, copper in round pieces, and coined silver as currency, but all valued in terms of that cloth . . . .

The *qadi* Abu ʿAbd Allah Muhammad b. ʿAbd al-Malik al-Marrakushi in his biographical dictionary called the *Takmila* ("Supplement") mentions Abu Ishaq Ibrahim al-Kanimi the poet and man of letters and relates of him that he said: "In the land of Kanim, or near to it, there appear to one walking by night objects like pots of distant fire but if he goes to catch up with them they go farther away; even though he were to run he would not reach them, but they stay before him. Sometimes stones have been thrown at them and reached their mark and struck sparks off them." This Muhammad al-Salaliji related to me as he saw it in the *Takmila* . . . .

This country lies between [the meridians of] Ifriqiya and Barqa, extending on the south [of these] until it is level with the Central Maghrib. It is a land of famine and austerity. The worst qualities there predominate; its conditions, and the conditions of its inhabitants, are harsh. The first man to establish Islam there was Hadi al-ʿUthmani who claimed descent from ʿUthman b. ʿAffan. It passed after him to the Yazanis, the descendants of Dhu Yazan. Justice is upheld in their country. They follow the school of the Imam Malik. They dress simply and are rigid in religion. They have built at Fustat, in Cairo, a Malikite *madrasa* where their companies of travelers lodge.

Chapter Ten: The kingdom of Mali and what appertains to it

Be it known that this kingdom lies to the south of the extreme west and adjoins the Atlantic Ocean. The king's capital there is the town of BYTY. This country is very hot. The means of subsistence are exiguous, the varieties of food few. The people are tall, with jet black complexion and crinkly hair. Their height is chiefly due to their [long] legs, not the structure of the trunk. Their king at present is named Sulayman, the brother of the sultan Mansa Musa. He controls, of the land of the Sudan, that which his brother brought together by conquest and added to the domains of Islam. There he built ordinary and cathedral mosques and minarets, and established the Friday observances, and prayers in congregation, and the muezzin's call. He brought jurists of the Malikite school to his country and there continued as sultan of the Muslims and became a student of religious sciences.

The ruler of this kingdom is he who is known to the Egyptians as king of Takrur. If he were to hear of this he would be disdainful for Takrur is but one of the provinces of his kingdom. He likes best to be called ruler of Mali, because that is the biggest province and that is the name by which he is best known. This king is the greatest of the Muslim kings of the Sudan. He rules the most extensive territory, has the most numerous army, is the bravest, the richest, the most fortunate, the most victorious over his enemies, and the best able to distribute benefits.

The provinces comprised in this kingdom are: Ghana, Zafun, Tirafka [or Tiranka], Takrur, Sanghana, BANBʿW, Zarqatabana, [BYTRA] Damura, Zagha, Kabura, Bawaghuri, and Kawkaw. The inhabitants of Kawkaw and BYTRA are tribes of Yartan. The province of Mali is the one where the king's capital, BYTY, is situated. All these other provinces are subordinate to it and the same name Mali, which is the name of the chief province of this kingdom, is given to them collectively. The kingdom comprises towns, villages, regions, and districts to the number of fourteen.

The truthful and trustworthy shaykh Abu ʿUthman Saʿid al-Dukkali, who lived at BYTY for 35 years and went to and fro in this kingdom, related to me that it is square, its length being four or more months' journey and its width likewise. It lies to the south of Marrakech and the interior of Morocco and is not far from the Atlantic Ocean. It extends in longitude from Muli to Tura on the ocean. It is all inhabited with few exceptions. Under the authority of the sultan of this kingdom is the land of Mafazat al-Tibr. They bring gold dust *(tibr)* to him each year. They are uncouth infidels. If the sultan wished he could extend his authority over them but the kings of this kingdom have learned by experience that as soon as one of them conquers one of the gold towns and Islam spreads and the muezzin calls to prayer there the gold there begins to decrease and then disappears, while it increases in the neighboring heathen countries. When they had learned the truth of this by experience they left the gold countries under the control of the heathen people and were content with their vassalage and the tribute imposed on them.

In the whole kingdom of this sovereign there is none who is given the title of "king" except the ruler of Ghana who is like a deputy to him even though he is a king.

To the north of Mali there are tribes of white Berbers under the rule of its sultan, namely: Yantasar, Tin Gharas, Madusa, and Lamtuna. They are governed by shaykhs, save Yantasar who are ruled successively by their own kings under the suzerainty of the ruler of Mali. There are also pagans owing obedience to him. Among them are some who eat human flesh. Some have accepted Islam and some persist in the heathen state. (This has been mentioned in the appropriate place).

The city of BYTY is extensive in length and breadth. Its length would be about a stage and its width the same. It is not encircled by a wall and is mostly scattered. The king has several palaces enclosed by circular walls. A branch of the Nile encircles the city on all four sides. In places this may be crossed by wading when the water is low but in others it may be traversed only by boat . . . .

The citizens drink water from the Nile or from excavated wells. All this country is verdant and hilly. The hills are covered with wild trees, their branches intertwining and their trunks extremely thick. One tree spreads out sufficiently to give shade to 500 horsemen . . . .

[Al-Dukkali] also said that in the territory of the infidels adjacent to their country the elephant is hunted by magic. This is literally true, not a metaphor. In all the countries, especially Ghana, sorcery is much employed. They are forever litigating before their king because of it, saying: "Such-a-one has killed my brother, or son, or daughter, or sister, by sorcery." The killer is sentenced to punishment by retaliation and the sorcerer is put to death.

The king of this realm sits in his palace on a big dais, which they call *banbi* (spelled with "b, n, b") on a big seat made of ebony like a throne and of a size for a very heavily-built sitter. Over the dais, on all sides, are elephant tusks one beside the other. He has with him his arms, which are all of gold—sword, javelin, quiver, bow, and arrows. He wears big trousers cut out of about twenty pieces which none but he wears. About 30 slaves stand behind him, Turks and others who are bought for him in Egypt. One of them carries in his hand a parasol of silk surmounted by a dome and a bird of gold in the shape of a falcon. This is borne on the king's left. His emirs sit around and below him in two ranks to right and left. Further away are seated the chief horsemen of his army. In front of him there stands a man to attend him, who is his executioner [or sword-bearer], and another called *shaʿir*, "poet," who is his intermediary between him and the people. Around all these are people with drums in their hands, which they beat. Before the kings are people dancing and he is pleased with them and laughs at them. Behind him two flags are unfurled, and before him two horses are tied ready for him to ride whenever he wishes.

Whoever sneezes while the king is holding court is severely beaten and he permits nobody to do so. But if a sneeze comes to anybody he lies down face to the ground to sneeze so that nobody may know of it. As for the king, if he sneezes all those present beat their breasts with their hands.

They wear turbans with ends tied under the chin like the Arabs. Their cloth is white and made of cotton that they cultivate and weave in the most excellent fashion. It is called *kamisiya*. Their costume is like that of the people of the Maghrib—*jubba*, and *durra'a* without slit. Their brave cavaliers wear golden bracelets. Those whose knightly valor is greater wear gold necklets also. If it is greater still they add gold anklets. Whenever a hero adds to the list of his exploits the king gives him a pair of wide trousers, and the greater the number of a knight's exploits the bigger the size of his trousers. These trousers are characterized by narrowness in the leg and ampleness in the seat. The king is distinguished in his costume by the fact that he lets a turban-end dangle down in front of him. His trousers are of twenty pieces and nobody dares to wear the same.

The king of this country imports Arab horses and pays high prices for them. His army numbers about 100,000, of whom about 10,000 are cavalry mounted on horses and the remainder infantry without horses or other mounts. They have camels but do not know how to ride them with saddles . . . .

The emirs and soldiers of this king have fiefs and benefices. Among their chiefs are some whose wealth derived from the king reaches 50,000 *mithqal*s of gold every year, besides which he keeps them in horses and clothes. His whole ambition is to give them fine clothes and to make his towns into cities. Nobody may enter the abode of this king save barefooted, whoever he may be. Anyone who does not remove his shoes, inadvertently or purposely, is put to death without mercy. Whenever one of the emirs or another comes into the presence of this king he keeps him standing before him for a time. Then the newcomer makes a gesture with his right hand like one who beats the drum of honor (*juk*) in the lands of Turan and Iran. If the king bestows a favor upon a person or makes him a fair promise or thanks him for some deed the person who has received the favor grovels before him from one end of the room to the other. When he reaches there the slaves of the recipient of the favor or some of his friends take some of the ashes which are always kept ready at the far end of the king's audience chamber for the purpose and scatter it over the head of the favored one, who then returns grovelling until he arrives before the king. Then he makes the drumming gesture as before and rises.

As for this gesture likened to beating the *juk*, it is like this. The man raises his right hand to near his ear. There he places it, it being held up straight, and places it in contact with his left hand upon his thigh. The left hand has the palm extended so as to receive the right elbow. The right hand too has the palm extended with the fingers held close beside each other like a comb and touching the lobe of the ear.

The people of this kingdom ride with Arab saddles and in respect of most features of their horsemanship resemble the Arabs, but they mount their horses with the right foot, contrary to everybody else.

It is their custom not to bury their dead unless they are people of rank and status. Otherwise those without rank and the poor and strangers are thrown into the bush like other dead creatures . . . .

When the king of this kingdom comes in from a journey a parasol and a standard are held over his head as he rides, and drums are beaten and guitars (*tunbur*) and trumpets well made of horn are played in front of him. And it is a custom of theirs that when one whom the king has charged with a task or assignment returns to him he questions him in detail about everything which has happened to him from the moment of his departure until his return. Complaints and appeals against administrative oppression are placed before this king and he delivers judgment upon them himself. As a rule nothing is written down; his commands are given verbally. He has judges, scribes, and government offices. This is what al-Dukkali related to me.

The emir Abu'l-Hasan 'Ali b. Amir Hajib told me that he was often in the company of sultan Musa, the king of this country, when he came to Egypt on the Pilgrimage. He was staying in [the] Qarafa [district of Cairo] and Amir Hajib was governor of Old Cairo and Qarafa at that time. A friendship grew up between them and this sultan Musa told him a great deal about himself and his country and the people of the Sudan who were his neighbors. One of the things he told him was that his country was very extensive and contiguous with the ocean. By his sword and his armies he had conquered 24 cities each with its surrounding district with villages and estates. It is a country rich in livestock—cattle, sheep, goats, horses, mules—and different kinds of poultry—geese, doves, and chickens. The inhabitants of his country are numerous, a vast concourse, but compared with the peoples of the Sudan who are their neighbors and penetrate far to the south they are like a white birth-mark on a black cow. He has a truce with the gold-plant people, who pay him tribute.

Ibn Amir Hajib said that he asked him about the gold-plant, and he said: "It is found in two forms. One is found in the spring and blossoms after the rains in open country. It has leaves like the *najil* grass and its roots are gold. The other kind is found all the year round at known sites on the banks of the Nile and is dug up. There are holes there and roots of gold are found like stones or gravel and gathered up. Both kinds are known as *tibr* but the first is of superior fineness and worth more." Sultan Musa told Ibn Amir Hajib that gold was his prerogative and he collected the crop as a tribute except for what the people of that country took by theft.

But what al-Dukkali says is that in fact he is given only a part of it as a present by way of gaining his favor, and he makes a profit on the sale of it, for they have none in their country; and what Dukkali says is more reliable.

Ibn Amir Hajib said also that the blazon of this king is yellow on a red ground. Standards are unfurled over him whenever he rides on horseback; they are very big flags. The ceremonial for him who presents himself to the king or who receives a favor is that he bares the front of his head and makes the *juk*-beating gesture towards the ground with his right hand as the Tatars do; if a more profound obeisance is required he grovels before the king. "I have seen this (says Ibn Amir Hajib) with my own eyes." A custom of this sultan is that he does not eat in the presence of anybody, be he who he may, but eats always alone. And it is a custom of his people that if one of them should have reared a beautiful daughter he offers her to the king as a concubine, and he possesses her without a marriage ceremony as slaves are possessed, and this in spite of the fact that Islam has triumphed among them and that they follow the Malikite school and that this sultan Musa was pious and assiduous in prayer, Koran reading, and mentioning God.

"I said to him (says Ibn Amir Hajib) that this was not permissible for a Muslim, whether in law or reason, and he said: 'Not even for kings?' and I replied: 'No! not even for kings! Ask the scholars!' He said: 'By God, I did not know that. I hereby leave it and abandon it utterly!'

"I saw that this sultan Musa loved virtue and people of virtue. He left his kingdom and appointed as his deputy there his son Muhammad and emigrated to God and His Messenger. He accomplished the obligations of the Pilgrimage, visited [the tomb of] the Prophet [at Medina] (God's blessing and peace be upon him!) and returned to his country with the intention of handing over his sovereignty to his son and abandoning it entirely to him and returning to Mecca the Venerated to remain there as a dweller near the sanctuary; but death overtook him, may God (who is great) have mercy upon him.

"I asked him if he had enemies with whom he fought wars and he said: 'Yes, we have a violent enemy who is to the Sudan as the Tatars are to you. They have an analogy with the Tatars in various respects. They are wide in the face and flat-nosed. They shoot well with [bow and] arrows. Their horses are crossbred with slit noses. Battles take place between us and they are formidable because of their accurate shooting. War between us has its ups and downs.'" . . . .

Ibn Amir Hajib continued: "I asked sultan Musa how the kingdom fell to him, and he said: 'We belong to a house which hands on the kingship by inheritance. The king who was my predecessor did not believe that it was impossible to discover the furthest limit of the Atlantic Ocean and wished vehemently to do so. So he equipped 200 ships filled with men and the same number equipped with gold, water, and provisions enough to last them for years, and he said to the man deputed to lead them: "Do not return until you reach the end of it or your provisions and water give out." They departed and a long time passed before anyone came back. Then one ship returned and we asked the captain what news they brought. He said: "Yes, O Sultan, we travelled for a long time until there appeared in the open sea [as it were] a river with a powerful current. Mine was the last of those ships. The [other] ships went on ahead but when they reached that place they did not return and no more was seen of them and we do not know what became of them. As for me, I went about at once and did not enter that river." But the sultan disbelieved him.

"'Then that sultan got ready 2,000 ships, 1,000 for himself and the men whom he took with him and 1,000 for water and provisions. He left me to deputize for him and embarked upon the Atlantic Ocean with his men. That was the last we saw of him and all those who were with him, and so I became king in my own right.'

"This sultan Musa, during his stay in Egypt both before and after his journey to the Noble Hijaz, maintained a uniform attitude of worship and turning towards God. It was as though he were standing before Him because of His continual presence in his mind. He and all those with him behaved in the same manner and were well-dressed, grave, and dignified. He was noble and generous and performed many acts of charity and kindness. He had left his country with 100 loads of gold that he spent during his Pilgrimage on the tribes who lay along his route from his country to Egypt, while he was in Egypt, and again from Egypt to the Noble Hijaz and back. As a consequence he needed to borrow money in Egypt and pledged his credit with the merchants at a very high rate of gain so that they made 700 dinars profit on 300. Later he paid them back amply. He sent to me 500 *mithqals* of gold by way of honorarium.

"The currency in the land of Takrur consists of cowries and the merchants whose principal import these are make big profits on them." Here ends what Ibn Amir Hajib said.

From the beginning of my coming to stay in Egypt I heard talk of the arrival of this sultan Musa on his Pilgrimage and found the Cairenes eager to recount what they had seen of the Africans' prodigal spending. I asked the emir Abu'l-'Abbas Ahmad b. al-Hak the *mihmandar* [the official in charge of receiving foreign ambassadors], who told me of this sultan's opulence, manly virtues, and piety. "'When I went out to meet him (he said), that is, on behalf of the mighty sultan al-Malik al-Nasir [whose third reign was 1309–40], he did me extreme honor and treated me with the greatest courtesy. He addressed me, however, only through an interpreter despite his perfect ability to speak in the Arabic tongue. Then he forwarded to the royal treasury many loads of unworked native gold and other valuables. I tried to persuade him to go up to the Citadel to meet the sultan, but he refused persistently, saying: 'I came for the Pilgrimage and nothing else. I do not wish to mix anything else with my Pilgrimage.' He had begun to use this argument but I realized that the audience was repugnant to him because he would be obliged to kiss the ground and the sultan's hand. I continued to cajole him and he continued to make excuses but the sultan's protocol demanded that I should bring him into the royal presence, so I kept on at him till he agreed.

"When we came in the sultan's presence we said to him: 'Kiss the ground!' but he refused outright saying: 'How may this be?' Then an intelligent man who was with him whispered to him something we could not understand and he said: 'I will make obeisance to God who created me!' then he prostrated himself and went forward to the sultan. The sultan half rose to greet him and sat him by his side. They conversed together for a long time, then sultan Musa went out. The sultan sent to him several complete suits of honor for himself, his courtiers, and all those who had come with him, and saddled and bridled horses for himself and his chief courtiers. His robe of honor consisted of an Alexandrian open-fronted cloak embellished with *tard wahsh* cloth containing much gold thread and miniver fur, bordered with beaver fur and embroidered with metallic thread, along with gold fastenings, a silken skull-cap with caliphal emblems, a gold-inlaid belt, a damascened sword, a kerchief [embroidered] with pure gold, standards, and two horses saddled and bridled and equipped with decorated mule[-type] saddles. He also furnished him with accommodation and abundant supplies during his stay.

"When the time to leave for the Pilgrimage came round the sultan sent to him a large sum of money with ordinary and thoroughbred camels complete with saddles and equipment to serve as mounts for him, and purchased abundant supplies for his entourage and others who had come with him. He arranged for deposits of fodder to be placed along the road and ordered the caravan commanders to treat him with honor and respect.

"On his return I received him and supervised his accommodation. The sultan continued to supply him with provisions and lodgings and he sent gifts from the Noble Hijaz to the sultan as a blessing. The sultan accepted them and sent in exchange complete suits of honor for him and his courtiers together with other gifts, various kinds of Alexandrian cloth, and other precious objects. Then he returned to his country.

"This man flooded Cairo with his benefactions. He left no court emir nor holder of a royal office without the gift of a load of gold. The Cairenes made incalculable profits out of him and his suite in buying and selling and giving and taking. They exchanged gold until they depressed its value in Egypt and caused its price to fall."

The *mihmandar* spoke the truth, for more than one has told this story. When the *mihmandar* died the tax office found among the property which he left thousands of dinars' worth of native gold which he had given to him, still just as it had been in the earth, never having been worked.

Merchants of Egypt and Cairo have told me of the profits which they made from the Africans, saying that one of them might buy a shirt or cloak or other garment for five dinars when it was not worth one. Such was their simplicity and trustfulness that it was possible to practice any deception on them. They greeted anything that was said to them with credulous acceptance. But later they formed the very poorest opinion of the Egyptians because of the obvious falseness of everything they said to them and their outrageous behavior in fixing the prices of the provisions and other goods which were sold to them, so much so that were they to encounter today the most learned doctor of religious science and he were to say that he was Egyptian they would be rude to him and view him with disfavor because of the ill treatment which they had experienced at their hands.

Muhannaʾ b. ʿAbd al-Baqi al-ʿUjrumi the guide informed me that he accompanied sultan Musa when he made the Pilgrimage and that the sultan was very open-handed towards the pilgrims and the inhabitants of the Holy Places. He and his companions maintained great pomp and dressed magnificently during the journey. He gave away much wealth in alms. "About 200 *mithqal*s of gold fell to me," said Muhannaʾ, "and he gave other sums to my companions." Muhammaʾ waxed eloquent in describing the sultan's generosity, magnanimity, and opulence.

Gold was at a high price in Egypt until they came in that year. The *mithqal* did not go below 25 dirhams and was generally above, but from that time its value fell and it cheapened in price and has remained cheap till now. The *mithqal* does not exceed 22 dirhams or less. This has been the state of affairs for about twelve years until this day by reason of the large amount of gold they brought to Egypt and spent there.

A letter came from this sultan to the court of the sultan in Cairo. It was written in the Maghribi style of handwriting on paper with wide lines. In it he follows his own rules of composition although observing the demands of propriety. It was written by the hand of one of his courtiers who had come on the Pilgrimage. Its contents comprised greetings and a recommendation for the bearer. With it he sent 5,000 *mithqals* of gold by way of a gift.

The countries of Mali and Ghana and their neighbors are reached from the west side of Upper Egypt. The route passes by way of the oases through desert country inhabited by Arab and then Berber communities until cultivated country is reached by way of which the traveler arrives at Mali and Ghana. These are on the same meridian as the mountains of the Berbers to the south of Marrakech and are joined to them by long stretches of wilderness and extensive desolate deserts.

The learned man Abu'l-Ruh 'Isa al-Zawawi informed me that sultan Mansa Musa told him that the length of his kingdom was about a year's journey, and Ibn Amir Hajib told me the same. Al-Dukkali's version, already mentioned, is that it is four months' journey long by the same in breadth. What al-Dukkali says is more to be relied on, for Mansa Musa possibly exaggerated the importance of his realm.

Al-Zawawi also said: "This sultan Musa told me that at a town called ZKRY he has a copper mine from which ingots are brought to BYTY. 'There is nothing in my kingdom on which a duty is levied,' (he said), 'except this crude copper which is brought in. Duty is collected on this and on nothing else. We send it to the land of the pagan Sudan and sell it for two-thirds of its weight in gold, so that we sell 100 *mithqals* of this copper for 66 2/3 *mithqals* of gold.' He also stated that there are pagan nations in his kingdom from whom he does not collect the tribute Muslims levy upon non-Muslims but whom he simply employs in extracting the gold from its deposits. The gold is extracted by digging pits about a man's height in depth and the gold is found embedded in the sides of the pits or sometimes collected at the bottom of them.

"The king of this country wages a permanent Holy War on the pagans of the Sudan who are his neighbors. They are more numerous than could ever be counted." . . .

Chapter Eleven: The kingdom of the Berber Mountains

In the land of the Sudan there are also three independent white Muslim kings who are Berbers; the sultan of Ahir [Air], the sultan of DMWShH, and the sultan of Tadmekka. The three are Muslim kings in the south of the west, between Morocco (the kingdom of the sultan Abu'l-Hasan) and the country of Mali and its neighbors. Each of them is an independent sovereign; no one of them rules another, but the greatest is the king of Ahir. They are Berbers and dress more or less like the Moroccans in the *durraʿa* (except that it is narrower) and turban with chin-band. Having no horses, they ride camels. Neither the Marinid sultan [of Morocco] nor the ruler of Mali has any authority over them. They live, as desert dwellers do, on meat and milk; grain is very scarce with them.

Shaykh Saʿid al-Dukkali told me that he passed through their country on one of his journeys but he did not remain long among them as they were short of food.

Zawawi told me that these Berbers possess inhabited mountains that produce many fruits. What is under the control of these three is about half of what the king of Mali possesses, or a little more. The latter enjoys a greater income because of his proximity to the land of the infidels, for the place where the gold sprouts is there and he can coerce them. His income is great for this reason and because of the abundance of the goods that are sold in his country and what he gains from forays into the lands of the infidels. The land of the former, on the contrary, is sterile and they have no opportunity to earn. They make their living principally from their animals.

12. A Famous World Traveler Visits Fourteenth-Century Mali and Pens a Detailed Report

IBN BATTUTA (1352-1353)

Ibn Battuta (1304–1368) is the only author in this collection who actually crossed the Sahara and visited Mali. This was the last of his many trips that took him to different parts of the Muslim world. His journey to Mali, between February 1352 and December 1353, seems to have been commissioned by the Moroccan sultan Abu 'Inan (1348–59). Ibn Battuta took leave from the sultan before his departure, and was recalled by the sultan from Takedda. On his return to Fez he went to see the sultan. The latter appointed a scribe, Ibn Juzzay, to write down Ibn Battuta's account, which he completed in December 1355, two years after Ibn Battuta's return from the Sudan. Ibn Juzzay was busy for an additional three months improving the text. He described his editorial job as follows (quoted from The Travels of Ibn Battuta, *translated by H.A.R. Gibb [Cambridge: Cambridge University Press, 1958], pp. 6–7):*

I have rendered the sense of the narrative of the Shaykh Abu 'Abd Allah [Ibn Battuta] in a language which adequately expresses the purposes that he had in mind and sets forth clearly the ends which he had in view. Frequently I have reported the words in his own phrasing, without omitting either root or branch. I have related all the anecdotes and historical narratives that he related, without applying myself to investigate their truthfulness or to test them.

Source: N. Levtzion and J.F.P. Hopkins, *Corpus of Early Arabic Sources for West African History* (Princeton: Markus Wiener Publishers, 2000 and 2006), pp. 282–303, passim.

He himself has adopted the soundest methods of authenticating those of them that are wholly acceptable, and has disclaimed responsibility for the rest of them by expressions that give warning to that effect. I have registered by means of vowel signs and diacritical points [the pronunciation of] those names of places and of men which offer difficulties, in order that it might be more useful in ensuring accuracy and fixing the orthography. I have expounded in detail all those I could expound of the non-Arabic names, since they are confusing to people by reason of their foreignness.

There are some similarities between the texts of Ibn Battuta and al-ʿUmari that are unlikely to be accidental. Al-ʿUmari had completed his work some seventeen years before Ibn Juzzay edited Ibn Battuta's account. It is not impossible that Ibn Juzzay, a learned scholar and an official scribe, was acquainted with al-ʿUmari's work and referred to it to enrich Ibn Battuta's narrative.

Ibn Battuta returned to Morocco from Takedda, where he received the order of the Moroccan sultan to return to Fez. We do not know whether he intended to proceed farther east. He does however refer to Borno as one of the destinations of the copper of Takedda. Ibn Battuta knew that the name of the king of Borno was Idris (see the account of al-Maqrizi below). Copper was also sent to a place called "Kubar" in the land of the infidels; this was probably Gobir in Hausaland, which was not yet converted to Islam.

Note Ibn Battuta's description of the "Nile," which descends from Timbuktu eastwards to Nubia and over the cataracts to Egypt.

Then we arrived at the capital, Fez (may God protect it!), and there they took leave of our lord [the sultan] (may God support him!) and set off with the purpose of travelling to the land of the Sudan. . . .

Anecdote

Then we reached the town of Iwalatan and the beginning of the month of Rabiʿ I after a journey from Sijilmasa of two whole months. It is the first district of the Sudan and the sultan's deputy there is Farba Husayn. *Farba* [spelled out] means "deputy." When we arrived there the merchants placed their belongings in an open space, where the Sudan took over the guard of them while they went to the *farba*. He was sitting on a carpet under a *saqif* [shaded portico] with his assistants in front of him with lances and bows in their hands and the chief men of the Masufa behind him. The merchants stood before him while he addressed them, in spite of their proximity to him, through an interpreter, out of contempt for them. At this I repented at having come to their country because of their ill manners and their contempt for white men. I made for the house of Ibn Baddaʾ, a respectable man of Sala to whom I had written to rent a house for me. He had done so. Then the *mushrif* [commercial supervisor of Iwalatan] who is called [the] *manshaju* [spelled out] invited those who had come with the caravan to receive his reception-gift [*diyafa*]. I declined to go but my companions entreated me urgently, so I went with those who went. Then the *diyafa* was brought. It was *anili* meal mixed with a little honey and yoghurt that they had placed in half a gourd made into a kind of bowl. Those present drank and went away. I said to them: "Was it to this that the black man invited us?" They said: "Yes, for them this is a great banquet." Then I knew for certain that no good was to be expected from them and I wished to depart with the pilgrims of Iwalatan. But then I thought it better to go to see the seat of their king.

My stay in Iwalatan lasted about 50 days. Its inhabitants did me honor and made me their guest. Among them was the *qadi* of the place Muhammad b. ʿAbd Allah b. Yanumur and his brother the *faqih* and teacher Yahya. The town of Iwalatan is extremely hot. There are a few little palm trees there, in the shade of which they sow watermelons. Their water comes from there sip by sip. Mutton is abundant there and people's clothes are of Egyptian cloth, of good quality. Most of the inhabitants there belong to the Masufa, whose women are of surpassing beauty and have a higher status than the men . . . .

A similar anecdote

When I resolved to travel to Mali (between which and Iwalatan there is a distance of 24 days' travelling for an energetic traveller) I hired a guide from the Masufa, since there is no need to travel in company because of the security of that road, and set off with three of my companions. That road has many trees. Its trees are of great age and vast size, so that a whole caravan may get shelter in the shade of one of them. Some of them have no branches or leaves, and yet the shade of the trunk is such that a man may get shelter in it. The interior of some of these trees has rotted away, so that the rainwater collects in it as though it were a well and people drink from the water in it. In some there are bees and honey, which people collect. I passed by one of these trees and found in its interior a weaver who had set up his loom in it and was weaving. I was astonished at this . . . .

Gourds grow very big in the land of the Sudan. They make bowls of them, cutting each one in half so as to make two bowls, and carve them elegantly. When one of them goes on a journey his male and female slaves, carrying his furnishings and the vessels from which he eats and drinks made of gourds, follow him.

The traveler in this country does not carry any supplies, [whether staple food] or condiment, nor any money, but carries only pieces of salt and the glass trinkets which people call *nazm* and a few spicy commodities. What please them most are cloves, mastic, and *tasarghant,* which is their incense. When he reaches a village the women of the Sudan bring *anili* and milk and chickens and *nabq* flour and rice and *funi* (which is like mustard seed, and *kuskusu* and *'asida* are made from it) and cowpea meal and he buys from them what he wants. But eating the rice is harmful to white men and *funi* is better.

After a journey of ten days from Iwalatan we reached the village of Zaghari. It is a big village inhabited by traders of the Sudan called Wanjarata with whom live a company of white men who are Kharijites of the Ibadi sect [probably traders from the oases of the northern Sahara] called Saghanaghu [spelled out]. The whites who are Sunnis of the Malikite school are called by them *turi*. From this place *anili* is imported to Iwalatan.

Then we departed from Zaghari and arrived at the great river that is the Nile and on which is the village of Karsakhu [spelled out]. The Nile descends from there to Kabara [spelled out] and then to Zagha [spelled out]. Kabara and Zagha have two sultans who owe obedience to the king of Mali. The people of Zagha are old in Islam. They are pious and interested in learning. Then the Nile descends from Zagha to Tunbuktu, then to Kawkaw (which two places we shall mention), then to the village of Muli [spelled out], then to the land of the Limiyyun (which is the last district of Mali), then to Yufi [spelled out]. Yufi is one of the biggest countries of the Sudan, and their sultan is one of their greatest sultans. No white man enters this country because they kill him before he reaches it. Then the Nile descends from there to the country of the Nuba (who are Christians), then to Dunqula [spelled out] (which is the biggest of their lands; its sultan is Ibn Kanz al-Din [actually, Kanz al-Dawla], and he embraced Islam in the days of [the Mamluk sultan of Egypt] al-Malik al-Nasir). Then it descends to the cataracts, which are the last district of the Sudan and the beginning of the district of Aswan of Upper Egypt.

I saw the crocodile in this place on the Nile, near to the shore looking like a little boat. One day I had gone to the Nile to accomplish a need when one of the Sudan came and stood between the river and me. I was amazed at his ill manners and lack of modesty and mentioned this to somebody, who said: "He did that only because he feared for you on account of the crocodile, so he placed himself between you and it."

Then we departed from Karasakhu and arrived at the River Sansara [spelled out], which is about ten miles from the capital of Mali. It is their custom to prevent people from entering it without authorization. I had written before this to the white community, of whom the chief members were Muhammad b. al-Faqih al-Gazuli and Shams al-Din b. al-Naqwish al-Misri, to ask them to rent a house for me. When I reached the afore-mentioned river I crossed it by the ferry without anyone preventing me. I arrived at the town of Mali, the seat of the king of the Sudan, and alight-ed at the cemetery. I arrived at the white quarter and sought Muhammad b. al-Faqih. I found that he had hired a house for me opposite his house, so I went there and his son-[or brother-]in-law, the *faqih*, the Koran reciter 'Abd al-Wahid brought a candle and food. Then on the morrow Ibn al-Faqih came with Shams al-Din b. al-Naqwish and 'Ali al-Zudi al-Marrakushi, who was a scholar. I met the *qadi* of Mali, 'Abd al-Rahman, who came to me. He was one of the Sudan, a respectable pilgrim of noble virtues, who sent to me a cow as his reception gift. I met the interpreter Dugha [spelled out], one of the respected and important Sudan, who sent me a bullock, and the faqih 'Abd al-Wahid sent me two sacks of *funi* and a gourd of *gharti*. Ibn al-Faqih sent me rice and *funi* and Shams al-Din also sent me a reception gift. They did their duty towards me in the most complete fashion, may God reward them for their good deeds.

Ibn al-Faqih was married to a cousin of the sultan and she used to seek us out with food and other things. Ten days after our arrival we ate a porridge made of something resembling taro called *qafi*, which they consider preferable to any other food. The next morning we were all sick. There were six of us, and one of us died. I went to perform the dawn prayer but fainted during it, so I asked one of the Egyptians for a purga-tive and he brought me something called *baydar*, which is the root of a plant. He mixed it with aniseed and sugar and stirred it in water. I drank

71

it and vomited up what I had eaten with much bile. God spared me from death but I was ill for two months.

The Sultan of Mali

He is the sultan Mansa Sulayman. *Mansa* means "sultan" and Sulayman is his name. He is a miserly king from whom no great donation is to be expected. It happened that I remained for this period without seeing him on account of my illness. Then he gave a memorial feast for our lord Abu'l-Hasan (may God be content with him) [the Moroccan sultan who reigned 1331–48], and invited the emirs and *faqih*s and the *qadi* and the *khatib*, and I went with them. They brought copies of the Koran and the Koran was recited in full. They prayed for our lord Abu'l-Hasan (may God have mercy on him) and prayed for Mansa Sulayman. When this was finished I advanced and greeted Mansa Sulayman and the *qadi* and the *khatib* and Ibn al-Faqih told him who I was. He answered them in their language and they said to me: "The sultan says to you: 'I thank God.'" I replied: "Praise and thanks be to God in every circumstance."

Their trivial reception gift and their respect for it

When I departed the reception gift was sent to me and dispatched to the *qadi*'s house. The *qadi* sent it with his men to the house of Ibn al-Faqih. Ibn al-Faqih hastened out of his house barefooted and came in to me saying: "Come! The cloth and gift of the sultan have come to you!" I got up, thinking that it would be robes of honor and money, but behold! It was three loaves of bread and a piece of beef fried in *gharti* and a gourd containing yoghurt. When I saw it I laughed, and was long astonished at their feeble intellect and their respect for mean things.

My speaking to the Sultan after this and his kindness towards me

After this reception gift I remained for two months during which the sultan sent nothing to me and the month of Ramadan came in. Meanwhile I frequented the *mashwar* ("council-place") and used to greet him and sit with the *qadi* and the *khatib*. I spoke with Dugha the interpreter, who said: "Speak with him, and I will express what you want to say in the proper fashion." So when he held a session at the beginning of Ramadan I stood before him and said: "I have journeyed to the countries of the world and met their kings. I have been four months in your country without your giving me a reception gift or anything else. What shall I say of you in the presence of other sultans?" He replied: "I have not seen you or known about you." The *qadi* and Ibn al-Faqih rose and replied to him saying: "He greeted you and you sent to him some food." Thereupon he ordered that a house be provided for me to stay in and an allowance be allotted to me. Then, on the night of 27 Ramadan, he distributed among the *qadi* and the *khatib* and the *faqih*s a sum of money that they call *zakah* and gave to me 33-1/3 *mithqal*s. When I departed he bestowed on me 100 *mithqal*s of gold.

The Sultan's sitting in his pavilion

He has a lofty pavilion, of which the door is inside his house, where he sits for most of the time. On the *mashwar* side there are three wooden arches covered with sheets of gold or gilded silver and beneath them three covered with sheets of gold or gilded silver. There are cloth curtains over them and when it is the day for his sitting in the pavilion the curtains are raised and it is known that he is in session. When he is sitting they hang out from the window of one of the arches a silken cord to which is attached a patterned Egyptian kerchief. When the people see the kerchief drums are beaten and trumpets are sounded and there come forth from the gate of the palace about 300 slaves, some carrying in their hands bows and others having in their hands short lances and shields. The lancers stand on the right and the left and the bowmen sit in the same way. Then two saddled and bridled horses are brought, with two rams, which they say are effective against the evil eye. When he is seated three of his slaves come out quickly and summon his deputy Qanja Musa and the *farariyya* [spelled out], who are the emirs, and the khatib and the faqihs come and sit in front of the bodyguard on the right and the left in the council-place. Dugha the interpreter stands at the gate of the council-place wearing fine garments of silk brocade and other materials, and on his head a turban with fringes which they have a novel way of winding. Round his waist he has a sword with a golden sheath and on his feet boots and spurs. No one but he wears boots on that day. In his hand he has two short lances, one of gold and the other of silver, with iron tips. The troops, governors, young men slaves, the Masufa, and others sit outside the council-place in a broad street where there are trees. Each *farari* has his followers before him with lances and bows, drums and trumpets. Their trumpets are made out of elephant tusks and their [other] musical instruments are made out of reeds and gourds and played with a striker and have a wonderful sound. Each *farari* has a quiver suspended between his shoulder blades and a bow in his hand and rides a horse. His companions are some on foot and some mounted. Inside the council-place beneath the arches a man is standing. Anyone who wishes to address the sultan addresses Dugha and Dugha addresses that man standing and that man standing addresses the sultan.

His sitting in council

He also sits on some days in the council-place. There is a dais under a tree there with three steps, which they call the *banbi*. It is upholstered with silk. Cushions are placed upon it and the *shitr* is erected. This is like a dome of silk having on it a golden bird the size of a falcon. The sultan comes out of a door in the corner of the palace with his bow in his hand and his quiver between his shoulders. On his head he wears a *shashiyya* [cap] of gold tied with a golden strap. It has extremities like thin knives and is more than a span long. His clothing consists for the most part of a furry red tunic of the European cloth that is called *mutanfas*. The singers come out in front of him with gold and silver stringed instruments in their hands and behind him about three hundred armed slaves. He walks slowly, with great deliberation, and sometimes halts. When he reaches the *banbi* he stands looking at the people, then he mounts gently, in the same way that the khatib mounts the pulpit. As he sits the drums are beaten and the trumpets are sounded. Three slaves come out quickly and summon the deputy and the *farariyya* and they enter and sit down. The two horses and the two rams with them are brought. Dugha stands at the door and the rest of the people are in the street under the trees.

The self-abasement of the Sudan before their king and their scattering of dust on themselves before him and other peculiarities

The Sudan are the humblest of people before their king and the most submissive towards him. They swear by his name, saying: "*Mansa Sulayman ki.*" When he calls to one of them at his sessions in the pavilion that we have mentioned the person called takes off his clothes and puts on ragged clothes, and removes his turban and puts on a dirty *shashiyya*, and goes in holding up his garments and trousers half-way up his leg, and advances with submissiveness and humility. He then beats the ground vigorously with his two elbows, and stands like one performing a *rak'a* to listen to his words.

If one of them addresses the sultan and the latter replies he uncovers the clothes from his back and sprinkles dust on his head and back, like one washing with water. I used to marvel how their eyes did not become blinded.

When the sultan says something in his session those present remove their turbans from their heads and listen attentively to his words. Sometimes one of them will stand before the sultan and mention the deeds that he has performed in his service, saying: "I did so-and-so on such-and-such a day and I killed so-and-so on such-and-such a day." Those who know the truth about this express their affirmation by seizing the string of the bow and releasing it as one does when he is shooting. When the sultan says to him: "You have spoken the truth" or thanks him, he removes his clothes and sprinkles himself with dust. This is good manners among them.

(Ibn Juzzay says: The Master of the Signature [a Moroccan court title] the *faqih* Abu'l-Qasim b. Ridwan (may God ennoble him) informed me that when al-Hajj Musa al-Wanjarati came as an ambassador from Mansa Sulayman to our lord Abu'l-Hasan (may God be content with him) and he went into the noble session, some of his people carried with him a basket of earth and he sprinkled dust on himself whenever our lord spoke kindly to him, just as he would have done in his own country.)

His action at the festival prayer and on festival days

At Mali I was present at the two festivals of the Sacrifice and the Breaking of the Fast. The people went out to the prayer ground, which is in the vicinity of the sultan's palace, wearing fine white clothes, and the sultan went mounted with a *taylasan* [shawl, head-scarf] on his head. The Sudan wear the *taylasan* only at festivals, with the exception of the *qadi* and the *khatib* and the *faqih*s, who wear it on other days. On the day of the festival they [the *qadi*, *khatib*, and *faqih*s] were in front of the sultan, crying "There is no God but God" and "God is most great." In front of him there were red insignia of silk. At the prayer ground a tent had been erected and the sultan entered and put himself in order. Then he came out to the prayer ground. The prayers and the sermon were accomplished, then the *khatib* descended and sat before the sultan and spoke to him at length. There was a man there with a lance in his hand conveying to the people in their language the words of the *khatib*. It was an exhortation and a reminder and praise for the sultan and urging the necessity of obedience to him and paying him his due. During the two festival days the sultan sits in the afternoon on the *banbi*. The bodyguard comes with remarkable weapons, such as quivers of gold and silver and swords decorated with gold and with scabbards of the same, and lances of gold and silver, and clubs of crystal. Next to him stand four emirs whisking away the flies and having in their hands silver ornaments resembling stirrups. The *farariyyu* and the *qadi* and the *khatib* sit according to custom. Dugha the interpreter comes with his four wives and his slave girls. There are about a hundred of these, with fine clothes and on their heads bands of gold and silver adorned with gold and silver balls. A seat is set up for Dugha and he sits on it and plays the instrument that is made of reed with little gourds under it, and sings poetry in which he praises the sultan and commemorates his expeditions and exploits and the women and slave girls sing with him and perform with bows.

With them are about thirty of his slave boys wearing red tunics of cloth and with white *shashiyyas* on their heads. Each one of them is girt with a drum that he beats. Then come his young followers who play and turn somersaults in the air as the Sindi does. In this they show unusual elegance and skill. They play with swords in the most beautiful way and Dugha [also] plays remarkably with the sword. At this the sultan orders him to be given a bounty and a purse is brought in which there are 200 *mithqal*s of gold dust. He is told what is in it publicly. The *farariyya* stand and twang their bows in thanks to the sultan. On the next day each one of them gives to Dugha a gift according to his rank. Every Friday, in the afternoon, Dugha goes through the same performance as we have mentioned.

An amusing story about the poets' reciting to the sultan

On the feast day, when Dugha has finished his performance, the poets come. They are called *jula* [spelled out], of which the singular is *jali* [*dyeli* in Mande]. Each of them has enclosed himself within an effigy made of feathers, resembling a [bird called] *shaqshaq*, on which is fixed a head made of wood with a red beak as though it were the head of a *shaqshaq*. They stand in front of the sultan in this comical shape and recite their poems. I was told that their poetry was a kind of exhortation in which they say to the sultan: "This *banbi* on which you are sitting was sat upon by such-and-such a king and among his good deeds were so-and-so; and such-and-such a king, and among his good deeds were so-and-so; so you too do good deeds which will be remembered after you." Then the chief of the poets mounts the steps of the *banbi* and places his head in the lap of the sultan. Then he mounts to the top of the *banbi* and places his head on the sultan's right shoulder, then upon his left shoulder, talking in their language. Then he descends. I was informed that this act was already old before Islam, and they had continued with it.

Anecdote

I was present at the sultan's session one day when one of their *faqih*s, who had arrived from a distant country, came and stood before the sultan and spoke to him at length. The *qadi* rose and said that he spoke the truth, then the sultan said that they spoke the truth. Each one of them took his turban from his head and sprinkled himself with dust in front of him. By my side there was one of the white men, who said to me: "Do you know what they said?" I said: "I don't know." He said: "The *faqih* has given the information that the locusts have fallen on their country. One of their righteous men went out to the place where the locusts were and was at a loss what to do and said: 'This is a lot of locusts.' A locust answered him and said:

'God sends us to the country in which there is much oppression in order to spoil its crops.'" The *qadi* and the sultan believed him and the latter said thereupon to the emirs: "I am innocent of oppression and any one of you who is oppressive I will punish. And if anybody knows of an oppressor and does not tell me of him, then the sin of that oppressor will fall upon his neck, and God will call him to reckoning!" When he spoke these words the *farariyya* took off their turbans and asserted their innocence of oppression.

Anecdote

One day I was present at the Friday service when a certain merchant, a Masufa scholar called Abu Hafs, stood up and said: "O people of the Mosque, I call you to witness that I call Mansa Sulayman to judgment before the Prophet of God (may God bless him and give him peace)!" When he said this a group of men came out from the sultan's box and said to him: "Who has done you wrong? Who has taken something from you?" He said: "The *manshaju* of Iwalatan" (meaning its *mushrif* or commercial supervisor). "He has taken from me something worth 600 *mithqals* and wishes to give me for it 100 *mithqals* only." The sultan sent for him at once and after some days he appeared and the two of them were referred to the *qadi*. The merchant's due was established, and he took it. Afterwards the *mushrif* was relieved of his office.

Anecdote

It happened during my sojourn at Mali that the sultan was displeased with his chief wife, the daughter of his maternal uncle, called Qasa. The meaning of *qasa* with them is "queen." She was his partner in rule according to the custom of the Sudan, and her name was mentioned with his from the pulpit. He imprisoned her in the house of one of the *farariyya* and appointed in her place his other wife Banju, who was not of royal blood. People talked much about this and disapproved of his act. His female cousins [literally, the daughters of his paternal uncle] went in to congratulate Banju on her queenship. They put ashes on their forearms and did not scatter dust on their heads. Then the sultan released Qasa from her confinement. His cousins went in to congratulate her on her release and scattered dust over themselves according to the custom. Banju complained about this to the sultan and he was angry with his cousins. They were afraid of him and sought sanctuary in the mosque. He pardoned them and summoned them into his presence. The women's custom when they go into the sultan's presence is that they divest themselves of their clothes and enter naked. This they did and he was pleased with them. They proceeded to come to the door of the sultan morning and evening for a period of seven days, this being the practice of anyone whom the sultan has pardoned.

Qasa began to ride every day with her slave girls and men with dust on their heads and to stand by the council place veiled, her face being invisible. The emirs talked much about her affair, so the sultan gathered them at the council place and said to them through Dugha: "You have been talking a great deal about the affair of Qasa. She has committed a great crime." Then one of her slave girls was brought bound and shackled and he said to her: "Say what you have to say!" She informed them that Qasa had sent her to Jatil, the sultan's cousin [literally, the son of his paternal uncle] who was in flight from him at Kanburni, and invited him to depose the sultan from his kingship, saying: "I and all the army are at your service!" When the emirs heard that they said: "Indeed, that is a great crime and for it she deserves to be killed!" Qasa was fearful at this and sought refuge at the house of the *khatib*. It is their custom there that they seek sanctuary in the mosque, or if that is not possible then in the house of the *khatib*.

The Sudan disliked Mansa Sulayman on account of his avarice.

80

Before him the king was Mansa Magha, and before Mansa Magha, Mansa Musa. Mansa Musa was generous and virtuous. He liked white men and treated them kindly. It was he who gave to Abu Ishaq al-Sahili in a single day 4,000 *mithqals*. Reliable persons have informed me that he gave to Mudrik b. Faqqus 3,000 *mithqals* in a single day. His grandfather Sariq Jata [perhaps Mari Jata of Ibn Khaldun] embraced Islam at the hands of the grandfather of this Mudrik.

Anecdote

This *faqih* Mudrik informed me that a man from Tlemcen called Ibn Shaykh al-Laban had made a gift to sultan Mansa Musa in his youth of seven *mithqals*. At that time Mansa Musa was a boy, without influence. Then it happened that when he had become sultan Mudrik came to him about a dispute. Mansa Musa recognized him and brought him so close to himself that he sat with him on the *banbi*. Then he made him admit the kindness that he had done to him and said to the emirs: "What should be the reward of one who has done the good deed that he has done?" They said: "For a kindness ten times the like thereof, so give him 70 *mithqals*." Thereupon he gave him 700 *mithqals* and a robe of honor and slaves of both sexes and ordered him not to cut himself off from him. The son of the aforementioned Ibn Shaykh al-Laban, who was a scholar teaching the Koran in Mali, also told me this story.

What I approved of and what I disapproved of among the acts of the Sudan

One of their good features is their lack of oppression. They are the farthest removed of people from it and their sultan does not permit anyone to practice it. Another is the security embracing the whole country, so that neither the traveler there nor dweller has anything to fear from thief or usurper. Another is that they do not interfere with the wealth of any white man who dies among them, even though it be *qintar* upon *qintar*. They simply leave it in the hands of a trustworthy white man until the one to whom it is due takes it. Another is their assiduity in prayer and their persistence in performing it in congregation and beating their children to make them perform it. If it is a Friday and a man does not go early to the mosque he will not find anywhere to pray because of the press of the people. It is their habit that every man sends his servant with his prayer-mat to spread it for him in a place that he thereby has a right to until he goes to the mosque. Their prayer-carpets are made from the fronds of a tree resembling the palm that has no fruit. Another of their good features is their dressing in fine white clothes on Friday. If any one of them possesses nothing but a ragged shirt he washes it and cleanses it and attends the Friday prayer in it. Another is their eagerness to memorize the great Koran. They place fetters on their children if there appears on their part a failure to memorize it and they are not undone until they memorize it.

I went into the house of the *qadi* on the day of the festival and his children were fettered so I said to him: "Aren't you going to let them go?" He replied: "I shan't do so until they've got the Koran by heart!" One day I passed a youth of theirs, of good appearance and dressed in fine clothes, with a heavy fetter on his leg. I said to those who were with me: "What has this boy done? Has he killed somebody?" The lad understood what I had said and laughed, and they said to me: "He's only been fettered so that he'll learn the Koran!"

One of their disapproved acts is that their female servants and slave girls and little girls appear before men naked, with their privy parts uncovered. During Ramadan I saw many of them in this state, for it is the custom of the *farariyya* to break their fast in the house of the sultan, and each one brings his food carried by twenty or more of his slave girls, they all being naked. Another is that their women go into the sultan's presence naked and uncovered, and that his daughters go naked. On the night of 25

Ramadan I saw about 200 slave girls bringing out food from his palace naked, having with them two of his daughters with rounded breasts having no covering upon them. Another is their sprinkling dust and ashes on their heads out of good manners. Another is what I mentioned in connection with the comic anecdote about the poets' recitation. Another is that many of them eat carrion, and dogs, and donkeys.

My departure from Mali

I had entered on 14 Jumada I 758/28 July 1352 and my departure from there was on 22 Muharram 754/27 February 1353. A merchant called Abu Bakr b. Ya'qub accompanied me. We took the road toward Mima. I had a camel which I was riding because horses are very expensive, each of them being worth 100 *mithqal*s. We arrived at a big channel issuing from the Nile, which may only be crossed in boats. This place has many mosquitoes and nobody passes there except by night. We reached the channel a third of the way through the night, which was moonlit . . . .

At this channel we stayed in a big village over which there is a governor of the Sudan, a worthy pilgrim called Farba Magha [spelled out]. He is one of those who made the Pilgrimage with the sultan Mansa Musa.

Anecdote

Farba Magha informed me that when Mansa Musa arrived at this channel he had with him a *qadi*, a white man whose *kunya* was Abu'l-ʿAbbas, known as al-Dukkali. He bestowed upon him 4,000 *mithqal*s for his expenses. When they reached Mima he complained to the sultan that the 4,000 *mithqal*s had been stolen from him from his house. The sultan summoned the emir of Mima and threatened him with death if he did not produce the one who had stolen them. The emir looked for the thief but found nobody, for no thief is to be found in that country, so he entered the *qadi*'s house and coerced his servants and threatened them. So one of al-Dukkali's slave girls told him: "He hasn't lost anything. He has just buried them with his own hands in that place." She indicated the place to him and the emir got them out and took them to the sultan and told him the tale. He was enraged with the *qadi* and banished him to the land of the infidels who eat mankind. He stayed among them for four years, and then he was returned to his own country. The infidels refrained from eating him simply because he was white, for they say that the eating of a white man is harmful because he has not matured. In their opinion the black man is the ripe one.

Anecdote

A group of these Sudan who eat humankind came with an emir of theirs to the sultan Mansa Sulayman. It is their custom to attach big earrings to their ears, the hole through each ring being half a span across, and envelop themselves in wraps of silk. The gold mine is in their country. The sultan did them honor and gave them a slave girl as part of his reception-gift. They slaughtered her and ate her and smeared their faces and hands with her blood and came in gratitude to the sultan. I was informed that their custom whenever they come in deputation to him is to do that, and I was told of them that they say that the tastiest part of women's flesh is the palms and the breast.

Then we set off from this village that is on the channel and reached the village of Quri [spelled out] Mansa. The camel that I used to ride died there. The man who was pasturing it told me about this so I went out to look into it and found that the Sudan had eaten it according to their custom of eating carrion. So I sent two youths whom I had hired for my service for them to buy me a camel at Zaghari, which was at a distance of two days' journey away. Some of the companions of Abu Bakr b. Ya'qub stayed with me while he went on to wait for us at Mima. I stayed for six days, during which a certain pilgrim of this village made me his guest, until the two youths arrived with the camel . . . .

Anecdote

Then I journeyed to the village of Mima [spelled out] and encamped at wells outside it, and then we traveled from there to the town of Tunbuktu [spelled out]. There are four miles between it and the Nile. Most of its inhabitants are Masufa, wearers of the *litham* [male face-veil], and their governor is called Farba Musa. I was present with him one day when he appointed one of the Masufa as emir over a group. He bestowed on him a garment and a turban and trousers, all dyed, and sat him on a shield and the chief men of his tribe raised him on their heads.

In this town there is the grave of the talented poet Abu Ishaq al-Sahili of Granada, known in this country as al-Tuwayjin; also there is the grave of Siraj al-Din b. Kuwayk, one of the important merchants of Alexandria.

Anecdote

When the sultan Mansa Musa made the Pilgrimage he stayed at gardens belonging to this Siraj al-Din at Birkat al-Habash outside Cairo, which is where the sultan stays. He needed money, so he borrowed some from Siraj al-Din and his emirs also borrowed from him. Siraj al-Din sent his agent with them to claim the money, but he remained in Mali, so Siraj al-Din went himself, with a son of his, to claim his money. When he arrived at Tunbuktu Abu Ishaq al-Sahili acted as host to him. It was fated that he should die on that night and people talked about it, suspecting that he had been poisoned. So his son said to them: "I ate that very same food with him. If there had been poison in it it would have killed us all. It is just that his time was up." The son arrived at Mali, claimed his money, and went back to the land of Egypt.

From Tunbuktu I travelled on the Nile in a small boat carved out of a single piece of wood. Each night we stayed in a village and bought what we were in need of in the way of wheat and butter for salt, spices, and glass trinkets. Then we reached a place whose name I have forgotten which had a worthy emir, a pilgrim called Farba Sulayman, well known for his courage and strength. Nobody is capable of drawing his bow. I did not see among the Sudan anybody taller or more heavily built than he. In this village I had need of a little sorghum, so I came to him. That was the day of the Prophet's birthday (may God bless him and give him peace) so I greeted him and he asked me about my coming. He had with him a *faqih* who wrote for him, so I took a board which was in front of him and wrote upon it: "O *faqih*, tell this emir that we are in need of a little sorghum for our traveling provisions. Peace be upon you." I handed the board to the *faqih* for him to read what was on it himself and then speak about it to the emir in his own tongue. But he read it out loud, and the emir understood and led me by the hand into his council room. There were many weapons there—shields, bows, and lances. I found with him *Kitab al-Mudhish* by Ibn al-Jawzi and began to read it. Then a drink of theirs was brought, called *daqnu* [spelled out], which is water containing sorghum meal mixed with a little honey or milk. They drink it instead of water because if they drink pure water it harms them. If they can find no sorghum they mix it with honey or milk. Then a green watermelon was brought and we ate some of it. A youth five spans high came in. He called to him, and he said to me: "This is your reception-gift. Guard him so he doesn't flee." I took him and wished to go, but he said: "Stay until food comes." There came to us a slave girl of his, an Arab girl from Damascus who spoke to me in Arabic. While this was going on we heard an uproar in his house, so he sent the slave girl to find out what it was about. She returned and told him that a daughter of his had died. He said: "I don't like weeping, so come, let's walk down to the river," by which he meant the Nile. He has houses on the bank. He brought a horse and said to me: "Ride!" I replied: "I shall not ride while you are walking." So we walked together and reached his houses on the Nile. Food was brought, and we ate. Then I took my leave of him and went away. I did not see among the Sudan anyone more generous or worthy than he. The lad whom he gave to me has remained in my possession till now.

Then I traveled to the town of Kawkaw, which is a great town on the Nile, one of the finest, biggest, and most fertile cities of the Sudan. There is much rice there, and milk, and chickens, and fish, and the *'inani* cucumber which has no like. Its people conduct their buying and selling with cowries, like the people of Mali. I remained there for about a month as a guest of Muhammad b. 'Umar of Miknasa. He was a witty, humorous and worthy man and died there after I had left. I was also the guest of al-Hajj Muhammad al-Wujdi al-Tazi, who was one of those who had been to the Yemen, and the *faqih* Muhammad al-Filali, the imam of the mosque of the whites.

Then I left there for Takedda by land in a big caravan of men from Ghadamis . . . .

The copper mine

The copper mine is outside Takedda. They excavate the earth for it and bring it to the town and smelt it in their houses. Their male and female slaves do this. When they have smelted it into red copper they make bars of it a span and a half long, some thin and some thick, of which the thick are sold at 400 bars per gold *mithqal* and the thin at 600 or 700 for a *mithqal*. This is their currency. With the thin ones they buy meat and firewood and with the thick ones male and female slaves, sorghum, butter, and wheat. The copper is transported from there to the city of Kubar [Gobir] in the land of the infidels and to Zaghay and to the land of Borno, which is at a distance of forty days from Takedda. The people of Borno are Muslims having a king named Idris who does not appear to the people and does not address them except from behind a curtain. From this country they bring handsome slave girls and young men slaves and cloth dyed with saffron . . . .

The sultan of Takedda

During my stay there the *qadi* Abu Ibrahim and the *khatib* Muhammad and the teacher Abu Hafs and the shaykh Sa'id b. 'Ali went to the sultan of Takedda, a Berber named Izar, who was at a day's journey distant. A dispute had arisen between him and the Takarkari [unidentified], who was also one of the sultans of the Berbers, so they had gone to make peace with them. I wished to meet him, so I hired a guide and went to him. The aforementioned persons informed him of my arrival and he came to me riding a horse without a saddle, as is their custom . . . . I stayed with them for six days, and each day he would send two roasted rams, in the morning and in the evening, and he presented me with a she-camel and ten *mithqals* of gold. I left him and returned to Takedda.

The arrival of the noble command

When I returned to Takedda the slave boy of al-Hajj Muhammad b. Sa'id al-Sijilmasi arrived with the command of our lord, the Commander of the Faithful, the Champion of Religion, the one who has trust in the Lord of the Worlds [Abu 'Inan Faris, sultan of Morocco 1348–59], ordering me to go to his lofty seat. I accepted and obeyed forthwith . . . .

13. An Arab Historian Uses West African Oral Traditions to Reconstruct the Dynastic History of Mali

IBN KHALDUN (1374-1394)

Ibn Khaldun is the best-known Arab historian. He was born in Tunis in 1332, and spent most of his life in the service of North African rulers. Toward the end of his life he moved to Egypt, where he died in 1406. His most famous work is the Introduction *(al-muqaddima) to his voluminous universal history. This work, known by its shorter title as* The Book of Examples *(Kitab al-ʿibar), was written in the years 1374–78; however, Ibn Khaldun continued to revise and update events in Mali until 1394.*

Ibn Khaldun is unique among the Arab authors in appreciating the value of historical traditions. He recorded the oral history of Mali from Shaykh ʿUthman, who visited Cairo in 1394. Ibn Khaldun was able to present a review of the history of the lands of the Sudan over a period of four centuries, from the hegemony of Ghana through the Almoravids' intervention and the interlude of the Susu (who are prominent in the oral traditions but do not appear in other Arab sources before Ibn Khaldun) to the rise of Mali. Other informants were al-Hajj Yunus, probably the resident translator for Mali in Cairo, and a qadi from Sijilmasa who had lived for many years in Kawkaw. Ibn Khaldun met him at Hunayn in Algeria in 1374–75. Ibn Khaldun was careful to ask his informants about the exact pronunciation of African names.

A critical analysis of Ibn Khaldun's text permits the following reconstruction of the genealogy of the kings of Mali:

Source: N. Levtzion and J.F.P. Hopkins, *Corpus of Early Arabic Sources for West African History* (Princeton: Markus Wiener Publishers, 2000 and 2006), pp. 323, 332–42.

89

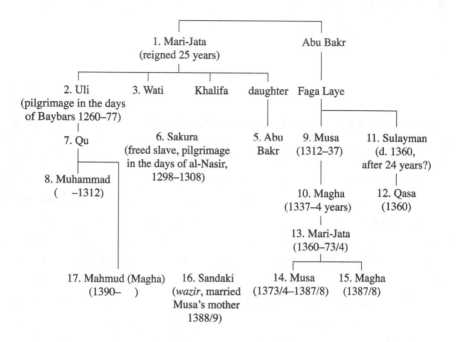

Ibn Khaldun's history gives an account of the exchange of diplomatic missions between Mali and Morocco. He was in Fez from 1354 to 1363, and witnessed himself the arrival there of the Malian mission during December 1360 or January 1361. He describes the excitement created by the gift of a giraffe that this mission brought to the Moroccan sultan.

The Pilgrimage of the king of the Takrur

. . . . The first among them to do so was Barmandar [*sic*]. I have heard from some of their eminent men that they pronounce his name Barmandana. The kings after him followed his example in performing the Pilgrimage.

Then Mansa Wali the son of Mari Jata went on the Pilgrimage during the reign of [the Mamluk sultan] al-Zahir Baybars [1260–77]. The next one among them on the Pilgrimage was Sakura, their freed slave, who had usurped their kingship. It was he who conquered the town of Kawkaw. Then he went on the Pilgrimage during the [second] reign of [the Mamluk sultan] al-Nasir [1299–1309]. After him Mansa Musa made the Pilgrimage, as is recounted in their history in dealing with the Berber dynasties, in the account of the Sanhaja and the dynasty of the Lamtuna, one of their peoples.

When Mansa Musa left the land of the Maghrib for the Pilgrimage he followed the desert route, and came out near the Pyramids in Egypt. He sent a rich present to al-Nasir. It is said that it included 50,000 dinars. Al-Nasir accommodated him at al-Qarafa 'l-Kubra and gave it to him as a fief. The sultan received him in his audience room, talked to him, gave him a gift, and supplied him with provisions. He gave him horses and camels, and sent along with him emirs to serve him until he performed his religious duty in the year 724/1324. On his return journey in the Hijaz he was stricken by a disaster from which his fate rescued him. It so happened that on the way he strayed from the *mahmil* and the caravan and was left alone with his people away from the Arabs. This route was completely unknown to them, and they could not find the way to a settlement or come upon a watering place. They went towards the horizon until they came out at Suez. They were eating fish whenever they could find some and the bedouin were snatching up the stragglers until they were saved.

The sultan then again bestowed honors upon him and was generous in his gifts. It is said that he had prepared in his country for his expenses a hundred loads of gold, each load weighing three *qintar*s. This was all exhausted, and he could not meet his expenses. He therefore borrowed money from the principal merchants. Among those merchants who were in his company were the Banu'l-Kuwayk, who gave him a loan of 50,000 *dinar*s. He sold to them the palace that the sultan had bestowed on him as a gift. He [the sultan?] approved it. Siraj al-Din b. al-Kuwayk sent his agent along with him to collect what he had loaned to him but the agent died there. Siraj al-Din sent another [emissary] with his son. He [the emissary] died but the son, Fakhr al-Din Abu Ja'far, got back some of it. Mansa Musa died before he [Siraj al-Din?] died, so they obtained nothing [more] from him . . .

The kings of the Sudan; a description of their circumstances, and a brief sketch of what has come to our knowledge concerning their dynasties

When Ifriqiya and the Maghrib were conquered [by the Arabs] merchants penetrated the western part of the land of the Sudan and found among them no king greater than the king of Ghana. Ghana was bounded on the west by the ocean. They were a very mighty people exercising vast authority. The seat of their authority was Ghana, a dual city on both banks of the Nile, one of the greatest and most populous cities in the world. It is mentioned by the authors of the *Book of Roger* [al-Idrisi] and the *Book of Routes and Realms* [al-Bakri].

The neighbors of Ghana on the east, as chroniclers assert, were another people known as Susu [with the letter *sad*] or Susu [with the letter *sin*] and beyond them another people known as Mali, and beyond them another known as Kawkaw or Kaghu, then beyond them another known as Takrur. I learn from Shaykh 'Uthman, the *faqih* of the people of Ghana and one of their chief men, and the most learned, religious, and celebrated of them, whom I met when he came to Egypt in [7]96/1394 in the course of the Pilgrimage with his family, that they call the Takrur "Zaghay" and the Mali "Ankariya." Later the authority of the people of Ghana waned and their prestige declined as that of the veiled people, their neighbors on the north next to the land of the Berbers, grew (as we have related). These extended their domination over the Sudan, and pillaged, imposed tribute and the poll tax, and converted many of them to Islam.

Then the authority of the rulers of Ghana dwindled away and they were overcome by the Susu, a neighboring people of the Sudan, who subjugated and absorbed them.

Later the people of Mali outnumbered the peoples of the Sudan in their neighborhood and dominated the whole region. They vanquished the Susu and acquired all their possessions, both their ancient kingdom and that of Ghana as far as the ocean on the west. They were Muslims. It is said that the first of them to embrace Islam was a king named Barmandana (thus vocalized by Shaykh 'Uthman), who made the Pilgrimage and was followed in this practice by the kings after him. Their greatest king, he who overcame the Susu, conquered their country, and seized the power from their hands, was named Mari Jata. *Mari*, in their language, means "ruler of the blood royal," and *jata* "lion." Their word for *hafid* ("servant" or "son-in-law") is TKN. I have not heard the genealogy of this king. He ruled for 25 years, according to what they relate, and when he died his son Mansa Wali ruled after him. In their language *mansa* means "sultan" and *wali* means "'Ali." This Mansa Wali was one of their greatest kings. He made the Pilgrimage in the days of al-Zahir Baybars. His brother Wati ruled after him and then a third brother, Khalifa. Khalifa was insane and devoted to archery and used to shoot arrows at his people and kill them wantonly so they rose against him and killed him. A grandson of Mari Jata, called Abu Bakr, who was the son of his daughter, succeeded him. They made him king according to the custom of these non-Arabs, who bestow the kingship on the sister and the son of the sister [of a former king]. We do not know his or his father's pedigree.

Their next ruler was one of their clients who usurped their kingship. His name was Sakura, pronounced Sabkara by the people of Ghana in their language, according to Shaykh 'Uthman. Sakura performed the Pilgrimage during the reign of al-Malik al-Nasir and was killed while on the return journey at Tajura. During his mighty reign their dominions expanded and they overcame the neighboring peoples. He conquered the land of Kawkaw and brought it within the rule of the people of Mali. Their rule reached from the ocean and Ghana in the west to the land of Takrur [sic] in the east. Their authority became mighty and all the peoples of the Sudan stood in awe of them. Merchants from the Maghrib and Ifriqiya traveled to their country. Al-Hajj Yunus, the Takruri interpreter, said that the conqueror of Kawkaw was Saghmanja, one of the generals of Mansa Musa.

The ruler after this Sakura was Qu, grandson of the sultan Mari Jata, then after him his son Muhammad b. Qu. After him their kingship passed from the line of Mari Jata to that of his brother Abu Bakr in the person of Mansa Musa b. Abi Bakr. Mansa Musa was an upright man and a great king, and tales of his justice are still told. He made the Pilgrimage in 724/1324 and encountered during the ceremonies the Andalusian poet Abu Ishaq Ibrahim al-Sahili, known as al-Tuwayjin. Abu Ishaq accompanied Mansa Musa to his country and there enjoyed an esteem and consideration which his descendants have inherited after him and keep to this day. They are settled in Walatan on the western frontier of their country.

On his return journey Mansa Musa was met by our friend al-Mu'ammar Abu 'Abd Allah b. Khadija al-Kumi, a descendant of 'Abd al-Mu'min [the Almohad ruler]. Mu'ammar had been a propagandist in the Zab for the Expected Mahdi [the Almohad founder] and had made raids upon the inhabitants of the Zab with guerilla bands of Arabs. The ruler of Wargalan had captured him by a ruse but released him after a time and he set off through the wilderness to seek from Mansa Musa forces with which to avenge himself. Having heard that Mansa Musa had set off on the Pilgrimage he stayed to wait for him in the town of Ghadamis in the hope of obtaining help against his enemy and support for his mission because of the power of Mansa Musa's authority in the desert adjacent to the territory of Wargalan. Al-Mu'ammar was well received and Mansa Musa promised him assistance in taking his revenge and invited him to accompany him to his country. Al-Mu'ammar, a truthful man, told me: "We used

94

to keep the sultan company during his progress, I and Abu Ishaq al-Tuwayjin, to the exclusion of his viziers and chief men, and converse to his enjoyment. At each halt he would regale us with rare foods and confectionery. His equipment and furnishings were carried by 12,000 private slave women wearing gowns of brocade and Yemeni silk."

According to al-Hajj Yunus, the interpreter for this nation at Cairo, this man Mansa Musa came from his country with 80 loads of gold dust, each load weighing three *qintars*. In their own country they use only slave women and men for transport but for distant journeys such as the Pilgrimage they have mounts.

Ibn Khadija continues: "We returned with him to the capital of his kingdom. He wished to acquire a house as the seat of his authority, solidly constructed and clothed with plaster on account of its unfamiliarity in their land, so Abu Ishaq al-Tuwayjin made something novel for him by erecting a square building with a dome. He had a good knowledge of handicrafts and lavished all his skill on it. He plastered it over and covered it with colored patterns so that it turned out to be the most elegant of buildings. It caused the sultan great astonishment because of the ignorance of the art of building in their land and he rewarded Abu Ishaq for it with 12,000 *mithqals* of gold dust apart from the preference, favor, and splendid gifts which he enjoyed."

There were diplomatic relations and exchanges of gifts between this sultan Mansa Musa and the contemporary Merinid king of the Maghrib, sultan Abu'l-Hasan. High-ranking statesmen of the two kingdoms were exchanged as ambassadors. The ruler of the Maghrib chose with care such products and novelties of his kingdom as people spoke of for long after (as will be mentioned in its place) and sent them by the hand of ʿAli b. Ghanim, the emir of the Maʿqil, and other dignitaries of his state. The successors of these two monarchs inherited these relations, as will be mentioned.

The reign of this Mansa Musa lasted for 25 years. On his death his son Mansa Magha succeeded him as ruler of Mali. Magha with them means "Muhammad." Mansa Magha died within four years of succeeding and was followed by Mansa Sulayman b. Abu Bakr, who was Musa's brother. His reign lasted 24 years, then he died and his son Qasa b. Sulayman succeeded him only to die nine months after his succession. After him ruled Mari Jata b. Mansa Magha b. Mansa Musa, whose reign lasted fourteen years. He was a most wicked ruler over them because of the tortures, tyrannies, and improprieties to which he subjected them. In [7]62/1360–61 he presented to the king of the Maghrib at that time, the sultan Abu Salim son of sultan Abu'l-Hasan, the gifts which are often mentioned, among which was that huge creature which provoked astonishment in the Maghrib, known as the giraffe. The people talked of it for long because of the various adornments and markings that it combined in its body and attributes.

The trustworthy *qadi* Abu 'Abd Allah Muhammad b. Wasul of Sijilmasa, who had settled in the land of Kawkaw in their country and had been employed as *qadi* there and whom I met at Hunayn in 776/1374–75, gave me a great deal of information about their kings which I wrote down. He told me about this sultan Jata, that he ruined their empire, squandered their treasure, and all but demolished the edifice of their rule. "His extravagance and profligacy," said Abu 'Abd Allah, "reached such a point that he sold the boulder of gold which was a prized possession of their treasury. It was a boulder weighing twenty *qintar*s that had been transported from the mine without being worked or purified by fire. They regarded it as the rarest and most precious of treasures because its like is so scarce in the mines.

"Jata, this profligate king, offered it to the Egyptian traders who travel back and forth to his country, and they bought it at a derisory price. In his loose living he squandered other royal treasures. He was stricken by sleeping sickness, a disease that often afflicts the inhabitants of that region, particularly the aristocracy. The victim suffers from attacks of sleepiness at all times until he hardly awakes except for short intervals. The disease becomes chronic and the attacks are continuous until he dies. This Jata was afflicted by this disease for two years and died in [7]75/1373–74.

"They appointed his son Musa to succeed him. He adopted a way of justice and moderation towards his people and quite abandoned the way of his father. Nowadays his advice is sought, but his vizier Mari Jata has seized his authority. (*Mari*, in their language, means "vizier" and *jata* has been explained above.) Mari Jata holds the sultan in seclusion and has taken his power exclusively into his own hands. He has seen to the mobilization of the army and the gathering of the squadrons. He has subdued the eastern provinces of their country and passed beyond the frontiers of Kawkaw. When he first assumed authority he sent against Takedda (which is in the country of the veil-wearers beyond Kawkaw) detachments that laid siege to it and invested it closely but then let it be. That is their situation at present.

"This Takedda [actually Tadmekka] is 70 stages from the town of Wargala towards the southwest. Its chief, who is of the wearers of the veil, is known as the sultan. The route of the pilgrims of the Sudan passes through his territory. He exchanges gifts and maintains diplomatic relations with the emirs of Zab and Wargala.

"The capital of the people of Mali is the town of BNY, an extensive place with cultivated land fed by running water, very populous with brisk markets. At present it is a station for trading caravans from the Maghrib, Ifriqiya, and Egypt, and goods are imported from all parts."

We have just heard that Mansa Musa died in the year [7]89/1387 and that his brother Mansa Magha succeeded him. Mansa Magha was killed after a year or so and was succeeded by Sandaki, the husband of Musa's mother (*sandaki* means "vizier"), but after a few months he was assassinated by a member of Mari Jata's family. Then there came forth from the land of the pagans beyond them a man named Mahmud, related to Mansa

97

Qu b. Mansa Wali b. Mari Jata the Great, who seized power and became ruler in [7]92/1390. His title is Mansa Magha . . . .

In the year [6]55/1257 there arrived [at Tunis, the Hafsid capital] gifts from the king of Kanim, one of the kings of the Sudan, ruler of Borno, whose domains lie to the south of Tripoli. Among them was a giraffe, an animal of strange form and incongruous characteristics . . . .

At a distance of twenty stages slightly to the west and south of this city [Wargala] is Takedda [Tadmekka], the capital of the veiled men's country and rendezvous for pilgrims of the Sudan. It was founded by veiled men of Sanhaja, who are its inhabitants at the present day. Its ruler is an emir of one of their leading houses and they call him sultan. There are diplomatic relations and exchanges of gifts between him and the emir of the Zab.

In the year [7]54/1353, in the days of sultan Abu 'Inan [of Morocco], I went to Biskara on royal business and there encountered the ambassador of the ruler of Takedda at the residence of Yusuf al-Muzani, emir of Biskara. He told me about the prosperous state of this city and the continual passage of wayfarers and said: "This year there passed through our city on the way to Mali a caravan of merchants from the east containing 12,000 camels." Another [informant] has told me that this is a yearly event. This country is subject to the sultan of Mali of the Sudan as is the case at present with the rest of the desert regions known as [the land of] the veiled men . . . .

[Hilal, chamberlain of Abu Tashfin, ruler of Tlemcen, went on the Pilgrimage.] He set sail in [7]24/1324 and disembarked at Alexandria. He went with the Pilgrims from Egypt in the party of the Commander [of the Caravan]. On the way he met the sultan of the Sudan from Mali, Mansa Musa, and a firm friendship grew up between them . . . .

The sultan's gift to the king of Mali of the Sudan bordering on the Maghrib

Sultan Abu'l-Hasan was well known for his ostentatious ways and his presumption to vie with the mightiest monarchs and adopt their customs in exchanging gifts with their peers and counterparts and dispatching emissaries to distant kings and far frontiers. In his time the king of Mali was the greatest of the kings of the Sudan and the nearest to his kingdom in the Maghrib. Mali was 100 stages distant over desert from the southern frontiers of his realms.

When Abu'l-Hasan took Tlemcen from the Banu 'Abd al-Wad in 737/1337, seized their authority, and conquered the realms of the central Maghrib, people talked of the affair of the beleaguering and death of Abu Tashfin [ruler of Tlemcen] and of the aggressiveness of the sultan and his contempt of the enemy and the news spread through all lands. So sultan Mansa Musa of Mali (who has been mentioned above in the appropriate section) aspired to correspond with him. Accordingly he deputed some of his subjects to go as emissaries with an interpreter drawn from the veiled men of Sanhaja who are the neighbors of his kingdom. They presented themselves before the sultan and congratulated him on his victory over his enemies. Abu'l-Hasan received them with honor, lodged them well, and sent them away fittingly. Desirous of displaying his customary opulence, he chose from his household treasury the rarest and most magnificent objects of Maghribi manufacture and appointed several of his courtiers, including the secretary of chancellery Abu Talib b. Muhammad b. Abu Madyan and his freedman 'Anbar the eunuch to convey them to the king of Mali [who was by then] Mansa Sulayman son [actually, the brother] of Mansa Musa, because his father [brother] had died before the return of his deputation. He also ordered certain of the desert Arabs of the Ma'qil to travel with them in both directions and this duty was undertaken by 'Ali b. Ghanim, emir of the Awlad Jar Allah of the Ma'qil, who accompanied them on their way in obedience to the sultan's command. This cortege set off across the desert and reached Mali after much effort and long privation. The king received them with honor and cordiality and dismissed them honorably. They returned to the one who had sent them accompanied by a deputation of Mali grandees who lauded his authority, acknowledged his rights, and conveyed to him that with which their master had charged them, namely [the expression of] humble submission and readiness to pay the sultan his due and act in accordance with his wishes.

Their mission being carried out, the sultan had achieved his aim of vaunting himself over other kings and exacting their submission to his authority and so he fulfilled God's due of thanks for His favor . . . .

[In 749/1348–49, following the conquest of Ifriqiya by Abu'l Hasan, several deputations converged on Constantine.] Among them also was a delegation from the people of Mali, kings of the Sudan in the Maghrib, who had been sent by their king Mansa Sulayman to offer congratulations on the dominion over Ifriqiya . . . .

The deputation of the Sudan, their gift, and the amazement that they provoked with a giraffe

When sultan Abu'l-Hasan sent to the king of the Sudan, Mansa Sulayman son of Mansa Musa, the gift which has been mentioned in its place, Mansa Sulayman occupied himself in preparing a comparable gift For this purpose he collected wonderful and strange objects of his country. Meanwhile Abu'l-Hasan died [in 752/1351] and by the time the gift had reached the furthest outpost of Mali at Walatan Mansa Sulayman had died [also about 760/1358–59].

Dissension now broke out among the people of Mali. Authority over them became divided and their [rival] kings tried to seize power. They killed each other and were preoccupied with civil war until finally Mansa Jata emerged and consolidated power in his hands. Examining the regions of his empire, he was told of the circumstances of this gift and was informed that it was at Walatan. He ordered it to be sent on to the king of the Maghrib and added to it a giraffe, a strangely-shaped and large-framed creature resembling various other animals.

They departed from their country and reached Fez in Safar [7]62/December 1360–January 1361. The day of their arrival was a memorable one. The sultan sat to receive them in the Golden Tower as he would for a review and criers summoned the people to go out to the open space outside the city. They came out, "hastening out of every mound" [Koran 21:36] until the space was too small for them and they climbed upon each other in the press round the giraffe in amazement at its form. The poets recited poems of eulogy and congratulation and description of the scene.

The deputation presented themselves before the sultan and delivered their messages affirming the affection and sincere friendship [of their king], apologizing for the slow arrival of the gift because of the dissension among the people of Mali and their struggle for power, praising their sultan and the state of their realm. During all this the interpreter was translating for them and they were twanging their bowstrings in approbation according to their approved custom. They greeted the sultan by scattering dust on their heads in conformity with the custom of non-Arab kings.

Then the king remounted and the assembly dispersed. Talk of it became widespread. The deputation continued to be entertained by the sultan, who died before their departure. His successor [Abu ʿUmar Tashfin, who succeeded in 1361], however, continued to give them hospitality until they departed for Marrakech and from there passed on to the territory of the Dhawi Hassan, Maʿqil Arabs who inhabit the [desert to the south of the] Sus and whose territory marches with that of the Sudan. And from there they rejoined their sultan.

14. A King of Borno Protests the Enslavement of His People by Arabs

AL-QALQASHANDI (1391-1418)

Al-Qalqashandi (1355–1418) was the author of a voluminous compilation, a manual for officials in the Mamluk chancellery, containing information about different states with which the Mamluks had diplomatic relations. He was concerned with the history of these countries, with their forms of government, and particularly with the formulae used in correspondence with their rulers. In the chancellery al-Qalqashandi had access to letters of correspondence between the king of Borno and the Mamluk sultan. In his letter the king of Borno complained about raids by the Judham Arabs. The latter were among the Arab tribes that penetrated from Egypt into the Sudan, where they pushed westward at the expense of Borno. The king of Borno believed that the Mamluk sultan had authority over these tribes. A civil war in the fourteenth century forced the king of Kanim to move his capital to Borno at the southwestern corner of Lake Chad. In the last paragraph al-Qalqashandi says that he has not found any correspondence from the king of Kanim; by that time Kanim had ceased to exist, and had been replaced by Borno.

The Land of Borno [spelled out as "al-Barnu"]

The inhabitants of Borno are Muslims and for the most part of black complexion . . . .

Source: N. Levtzion and J.F.P. Hopkins, *Corpus of Early Arabic Sources for West African History* (Princeton: Markus Wiener Publishers, 2000 and 2006), pp. 344–49.

The capital of the people of Borno is Kaka, according to what was told to me by the emissary of their sultan who arrived in Egypt in company with the pilgrims during the reign of the sultan al-Zahir Barquq [r. 1382–98] . . .

Another of their cities is Kutniski. It lies one day's journey to the east of Kaka.

There arrived a letter from the king of Borno towards the end of al-Zahir Barquq's reign in which the king mentioned that he was descended from Sayf b. Dhi Yazan. But he did not establish the genealogy, for he said [also] that he was of Quraysh, which is an error on their part, for Sayf b. Dhi Yazan descended from the *tubba's* of the Yemen, who were Himyarites. This will be mentioned below when we speak of correspondence, in the fourth *maqala* [unit of this book], if God wills. . . .

The ruler of Borno has also received correspondence from the sultan's court in Egypt, which will be mentioned there, if God wills . . .

I have seen in the formulary bearing the name of 'Ala' al-Din b. Fadl Allah that the correspondence of [the ruler of Borno] is on "third" sized paper. The validation is "his brother" and his designation "ruler of Borno."

During the reign of al-Zahir Barquq a letter arrived from this king [of Borno] in which he complained of the Judham Arabs who were his neighbors. He said that they had captured a group of his relatives and sold them abroad. He asked that inquiries should be made about them and that it should be forbidden to sell them in Egypt or Syria. He sent with the letter a suitable gift of mercury and other things. A reply was written by the hand of Zayn al-Din Tahir, one of the secretaries in the Palace of Justice. Its preamble read . . . It was dispatched by way of the ambassador who had come in company with the pilgrims. It was returned after a year or two with the reply written on the back . . .

On the correspondence emanating from the ruler of Borno [al-Barnu]

The form of his correspondence is that it is written on square paper in a hand like that of the Maghribis and if any of the correspondence is left over it is written on the back. The correspondence is opened with an opening address of praise to God; then it proceeds to the subject matter [of the letter] with the phrase "and after that" and completes it. I saw that he closed his correspondence addressed to the sultan's court by saying "peace be upon those who follow the Right Way." It would appear that that was ignorance on the part of the secretary of the rules of the secretarial art, since they have no guidance as to the correct ones.

This is the text of a letter which came to al-Malik al-Zahir Abu Sa'id Barquq. It arrived during 794/1391–92 in charge of the ruler of Borno's cousin with a present. It was prompted by what is mentioned in it concerning the Arabs of Judham who are his neighbors. It is written on square paper with lines side by side in a Maghribi hand, without margin at head or side. The conclusion of the letter is written on the verso, at the foot of the page:

"In the name of God, the Merciful, the Compassionate . . .

"From him who trusts in God (who is exalted), the most mighty king, the sword of Islam . . . Abu 'Amr 'Uthman the king, son of al-Hajj Idris the lamented *Amir al-Mu'minin* (may God ennoble his tomb and perpetuate his descendants in his kingship). These words come by the tongue of our secretary, who is of our family—without boasting:

"To the mighty King of Egypt, God's blessed land, Mother of the World: "Upon you be peace more fragrant than pungent musk, sweeter than the water of cloud and ocean . . .

"To proceed: We sent to you our ambassador, my cousin, whose name is Idris b. Muhammad, because of the misfortune which we and our vassal kings have experienced. For the Arabs who are called Judham and others have snatched away some of our free people, women and children, infirm men, relations of ours, and other Muslims. Some of these Arabs are polytheists and deviate from true religion. They have raided the Muslims and done great slaughter among them because of a dispute that has occurred between our enemies and us. As a result of this dispute they have killed our king 'Amr the Martyr b. Idris, the son of our father al-Hajj Idris son of al-Hajj Ibrahim. We are the sons of Sayf b. Dhi Yazan, the father of our tribe, the Arab, the Qurayshite; thus do we register our pedigree as handed down by our shaykhs. These Arabs have devastated all our country, the whole of Borno, up to this day. They have seized our free men and our relatives, who are Muslims, and sold them to the slave dealers of Egypt and Syria and others; some they have kept for their own service.

"Now God has placed the control of Egypt from the sea to Aswan in your hands. These our people have been seized as merchandise, so pray send to all your territory, your emirs, ministers, judges, magistrates, jurists, market overseers, that they may look and search and discover. If they find them, let them snatch them from their hands and put them to the test. If they say: 'We are free, we are Muslims,' believe them. Do not take them for liars. When the truth is clear to you release them. Restore them to their freedom and Islam. For certain Arabs cause mischief in our land and do not act righteously. They are those who are ignorant of the Book of God and the Sunna of His Messenger. They embellish that which is worthless. So beware of God, fear Him, and do not abandon them to be enslaved and sold. God (who is exalted) said: 'And the believers, men and women, are protecting friends of one another; they command the right and forbid the wrong.' And God (who is exalted) said to His Prophet (peace be upon him): 'So judge between them by that which God hath revealed and follow not their desires.' And God (who is exalted) said: 'And if God had not repelled some men by others the earth would have been corrupted.' He [the Prophet] (peace be upon him) used to say: 'The sultan is God's shadow upon earth to whom everyone resorts who has suffered wrong.' And he said: 'The Muslims are like a building; they will bind each other till the Day of Judgment.' And he said: 'The believer is the believer's brother; he will not wrong him nor forsake him,' etc. It says in *al-Hikma* [the title of an unidentified book]: 'It is a duty to enjoin the right on everyone who is vouchsafed authority on earth (by which he meant sultans), and on those who are within reach of it (by which he meant judges, governors, and emirs). If he cannot [command it], then [let him enjoin it] with his tongue (by which he meant faqihs and scholars); if he cannot, then with his heart (by which he meant the generality of Muslims).'

"May God prolong your days in the land. Restrain the Arabs from their debauchery. God (who is exalted) said: 'As for those who strive in us, we surely guide them to our paths, and lo! God is with the good.' He [the Prophet] (peace be upon him) said: 'Each of you is a shepherd, and each of you is responsible for his flock.' It says in *al-Hikma*: 'But for the sultan you would eat each other.' And he (who is exalted) said to his Prophet David (peace be upon him): 'O David! Lo! We have set thee as a viceroy upon the earth; therefore judge aright between mankind, and follow not desire that it beguile thee from the way of God. Lo! Those who wander from the way of God have an awful doom, forasmuch as they forgot the Day of Reckoning.'

"Peace be upon those who follow the right way."

It is undated.

On the correspondence emanating from the king of the Kanim

I have not found any correspondence of his but it is likely that correspondence from him is similar to correspondence from the ruler of Borno, for he is near to his kingdom. And God knows best.

15. The Saifawa Dynasty of Fourteenth-Century Kanim-Borno

AL-MAQRIZI(?) (c. 1397)

A fragment entitled "An Epistle on the Races of the Sudan," attributed to al-Maqrizi, was edited by Hamaker in 1820. It includes important information about Kanim and Borno. The latest date in this text is the year 800/1397–98. When this information is collated with data provided by Ibn Battuta and al-Qalqashandi it is possible to reconstruct a genealogy of the kings of the Saifawa dynasty of Kanim-Borno over the three generations that cover the whole of the fourteenth century.

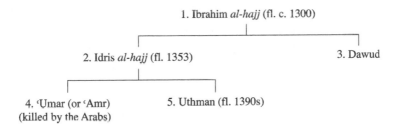

1. Ibrahim *al-hajj* (fl. c. 1300)

2. Idris *al-hajj* (fl. 1353)   3. Dawud

4. ʿUmar (or ʿAmr)   5. Uthman (fl. 1390s)
(killed by the Arabs)

According to the sixteenth-century chronicle of Ibn Furtu, Kanim was abandoned during the reign of Dawud b. Ibrahim (about 1366–76). According to the Diwan Salatin Burnu *it was during the reign of ʿUmar b. Idris (about 1382–87). According to the letter copied by al-Qalqashandi, the Judham Arabs killed ʿUmar.*

Source: N. Levtzion and J.F.P. Hopkins, *Corpus of Early Arabic Sources for West African History* (Princeton: Markus Wiener Publishers, 2000 and 2006), pp. 353–55.

The races of the Sudan

. . . [The Kanim are a numerous] people among whom Islam predominates. Their city is Aljama. The first of their kings to adopt Islam was Muhammad b. Jabal b. ʿAbd Allah b. ʿUthman b. Muhammad b. ʿBY—. They assert that he is descended from Sayf b. Dhi Yazan and that between the two there were about 40 kings. This king is a wandering bedouin. When he sits on his throne his subjects make obeisance to him and fall on their faces. His armies, including cavalry, infantry, and porters, number 100,000. Between Aljama and Yalamlam there dwell many unbelievers. The king of Aljama, i.e. the king of Kanim, has five [minor] kings under his sway. Their horses are small. Kanim is a vast region through which the blessed Nile flows . . . .

Their king in about 700/1300 was al-Hajj Ibrahim of the posterity of Sayf b. Dhi Yazan. He held the throne of Kanim. Kanim is the throne of Borno. There ruled after him his son al-Hajj Idris, then his brother Daʾud b. Ibrahim, then ʿUmar the son of his brother al-Hajj Idris, then his brother ʿUthman b. Idris who ruled a little before 800/1397–98. The people of Kanim then rose against them and apostatized and . . . . They are Muslims and wage Holy War on the people of Kanim. They have twelve kingdoms.

16. Fourteenth-Century Malian Kings Patronize the Eminent Andalusian Architect and Intellectual Abu Ishaq al-Tuwayjin

AL-MAQQARI (1591–1632)

Al-Maqqari was born in Tlemcen ca. 1591–92 and died in Cairo in 1632. His Nafh al-Tib *is a compilation of historical and biographical material from earlier sources related to Muslim Spain. The text quoted below includes three contemporary accounts from the fourteenth century concerning the Andalusian architect who accompanied Mansa Musa back to Mali and died at Timbuktu.*

[Chapter V: On those Andalusians who traveled to the East]

"Among them was Abu Ishaq al-Sahili, known as al-Tuwayjin or al-Tuwayjan, the celebrated scholar, the upright man for whom thanks are given, the renowned poet, a native of Granada from a family of rectitude, wealth, and trust. His father was the head of the perfumers' guild in Granada. As well as being head [of the guild] he was a scholar and lawyer, proficient and versatile. He was well versed in the law of inheritance.

"In his youth this Abu Ishaq was a notary in the lawyers' street of Granada. He departed from al-Andalus for the East and made the Pilgrimage and then travelled to the land of the Sudan. He made his home there and found high favor with its sultan. He died there, may God have mercy upon him." Here ends a summary of the words of the emir Ibn

Source: N. Levtzion and J.F.P. Hopkins, *Corpus of Early Arabic Sources for West African History* (Princeton: Markus Wiener Publishers, 2000 and 2006), pp. 370–71.

al-Ahmar in his book, *Nathir al-Juman fi man nazamani wa-iyyahu al-zaman*.

Abu'l-Makarim Mindil b. Ajurrum said: "It was related to me by one whose words may be trusted that the death of Abu Ishaq al-Tuwayjin took place on Monday 27 Jumada II 745/15 October 1346 at Tunbuktu, a place in the desert which is one of the provinces of Mali, may God have mercy on him." Then he vocalized al-Tuwayjin with "i" after the "j" and said: "This is how he vocalized it with his own hand, may God have mercy on him. Those who call him al-Sahili name him after his maternal grandfather."

Among them was the excellent imam, the litterateur Abu Ishaq Ibrahim b. Muhammad al-Sahili al-Gharnati. Al-ʿIzz b. Jamaʿa [the Shafiʿi *qadi* of Cairo, d. 1366] says: "He came to us from the Maghrib in the year 724/1324 then returned to the Maghrib in that year. We have heard that he died at Marrakech in the 740s/1340s."

Mali became known in Egypt through the spectacular visit to Cairo of Mansa Musa on his way to and from Mecca. So impressive was this visit that it was recorded as one of the major events of the year 724/1324 by Egyptian chroniclers of the fourteenth and fifteenth centuries, including the authors of the following four selections (see also selections 11, 12, 13, and 16). These historians recorded also other Takruri pilgrims.

17. Economic Aspects of *Mansa* Musa's Visit to Cairo, According to Various Named Informants

IBN AL-DAWADARI (1331-1335)

Ibn al-Dawadari wrote the history of the Muslim dynasties in nine volumes between 1331 and 1335, that is, he wrote less than ten years after Mansa Musa's visit to Cairo. He obtained some details about the kingdom of Mali from informants whom he mentions by name. This information should be compared with that of his contemporary al-'Umari. Ibn al-Dawadari has two pieces of information of political significance. One is that the 'Abbasid caliph, who was resident in Cairo as a puppet of the Mamluk sultans, girded Mansa Musa with a sword. In later years the Tarikhs of Timbuktu would have similar accounts concerning Askiya Muhammad of Songhay, that the 'Abbasid Caliph girded him with a sword, when he visited Cairo at the end of the fifteenth century. The

Source: N. Levtzion and J.F.P. Hopkins, *Corpus of Early Arabic Sources for West African History* (Princeton: Markus Wiener Publishers, 2000 and 2006), pp. 250–51.

second piece of information, which is unconfirmed by any other source, is that Mansa Musa undertook that the khutba *(sermon) and the coinage in Mali would be in the name of the Mamluk sultan. Both are signs of formal political submission to a sovereign.*

In this year 724/1324 the king of the Takrur arrived making for the Noble Hijaz. His name was Abu Bakr b. Musa [elsewhere Musa b. Abu Bakr]. He remained in Egypt for a year before betaking himself to the Hijaz. He had much gold with him. His is the country that puts forth gold.

I heard the *qadi* Fakhr al-Din, Inspector of the (victorious) Army say: "I asked the king of the Takrur: 'How is the description of the place where the gold grows with you?' He replied: 'It is not in that part of our land which belongs to the Muslims, but in the land which belongs to the Christians [*sic*] of the Takrur. We dispatch [collectors] to take from them a species of tribute due to us and obligatory upon them. These are special lands which put forth gold in this fashion: it consists of small pieces of varying sizes, some like little rings, some like carob seeds, and the like.'"

The *qadi* Fakhr al-Din continued: "I said: 'Why don't you take this land by conquest?' He replied: 'If we conquer them and take it, it does not put forth anything. We have done this in many ways but seen nothing there; but when it returns to them it puts forth as usual. This is a most amazing thing and is perhaps due to an increase in the oppressiveness of the Christians.'"

Then the king of the Takrur and his followers bought all kinds of things from New and Old Cairo. They thought that their money was inexhaustible. When they became immersed in buying and found that there was no limit to the different commodities in this country and they saw every day something better than the last, the money that they had with them gave out and they needed to borrow. Avaricious people lent to them in the hope of big profits on their return, but everything they had borrowed fell back on the heads of the lenders and they got nothing back.

Among these was our friend the shaykh and imam Shams al-Din b. Tazmart al-Maghribi. He lent them gold of good form but none of it came back. Then these people became amazed at the ampleness of this country and how their money had been used up without their having been able to complete the purchases they desired. So they became needy and resold what they had bought at half its value, and people made good profits out of them. And God knows best.

Our lord was very generous towards them and invested the king with a royal robe of honor by his authority, while the caliph girded him with a sword by his authority. He undertook that the *khutba* in his country should be in the name of our lord the sultan and the coinage likewise. Such an undertaking was never given to a ruler of Egypt except our lord the sultan [al-Nasir] (may his victories be mighty).

18. Problems of Diplomatic Protocol during *Mansa* Musa's Visit to Cairo

IBN KATHIR (c. 1350)

Ibn Kathir (1300–74) was Syrian, one of the principal historians of the Mamluk period. He wrote his history in about 1350. According to him Mansa Musa was young and handsome, which is the only information about Mansa Musa's age during the pilgrimage. Other details of his account must be compared with other versions of Mansa Musa's visit.

In the year [724] on 25 Rajab [18 July 1324] the king of the Takrur came to Cairo for the Pilgrimage. He camped at al-Qarafa. He had with him about 20,000 Maghribis and slaves. They had so much gold with them that the rate of gold fell by two dirhams in each *mithqal*.

He was called al-Malik al-Ashraf Musa b. Abu Bakr. He was a young handsome man. He had a vast kingdom that was three years' traveling [in extent]. It is said that there were 24 kings under his authority, each having people and soldiers under him.

When he entered the Citadel to salute the sultan he was ordered to kiss the ground, but he refused to do so. The sultan treated him with honor but he could not sit before he left the presence of the sultan. He was given a gray horse, with a covering of yellow satin. They prepared for him camels and much equipment befitting one like him. He also sent many presents to the sultan, including 40,000 *dinars*, and to the [sultan's] deputy he sent about 10,000 *dinars* and many gifts.

Source: N. Levtzion and J.F.P. Hopkins, *Corpus of Early Arabic Sources for West African History* (Princeton: Markus Wiener Publishers, 2000 and 2006), p. 305.

19. Diverse Notes on the Pilgrimage of *Mansa* Musa and Other West African Leaders

AL-MAQRIZI (1364-1442)

Al-Maqrizi (1364–1442) was one of the most famous historians of the Mamluk period. He studied with Ibn Khaldun when the latter was resident in Cairo in the years 1382–1406. The texts below are drawn from three different works by al-Maqrizi. The first text is a detailed account of Mansa Musa in a treatise devoted to kings who made the Pilgrimage. The second is from al-Maqrizi's work on the topography of Cairo, in which he refers also to a madrasa *endowed in the middle of the thirteenth century for the use of pilgrims from Kanim. The third text is from al-Maqrizi's annals, in which events are recorded in sequence. There are three references to the pilgrimage in the year 724/1324; Mansa Musa arrived in Cairo on 19 July, the pilgrims' caravan which he joined departed three months later on 18 October, and it returned on 27 December. There are at least five additional entries referring to pilgrims from West Africa (Takrur). On two occasions there was a king in the pilgrims' caravans. All the pilgrims' caravans brought slaves and gold.*

The kings of the Takrur who made the Pilgrimage:
Mansa Musa, king of the Takrur

The first of the kings of the Takrur to make the Pilgrimage was Saraban-dana or Baramandana. Then Mansa Wali son of Mari Jata did so in the

Source: N. Levtzion and J.F.P. Hopkins, *Corpus of Early Arabic Sources for West African History* (Princeton: Markus Wiener Publishers, 2000 and 2006), pp. 351–53, 355-56.

days of al-Malik al-Zahir Baybars; then Sakura, who had usurped their throne and conquered the land of Kawkaw; then Mansa Musa.

Mansa Musa arrived in Egypt in 724/1324 with magnificent gifts and much gold. The sultan al-Malik al-Nasir b. Qalawun sent the *mihmandar* to receive him and Musa rode to the Citadel on the day of his official reception. He refused to kiss the ground and said to the interpreter: "I am a man of the Maliki school and do not prostrate myself before any but God." So the sultan excused him and drew him near to him and did him honor. The sultan asked him the reason for his coming and he replied: "I wish to make the Pilgrimage." So the sultan ordered the *wazir* to equip him with everything he might need.

It is said that he brought with him 14,000 slave girls for his personal service. The members of his entourage proceeded to buy Turkish and Ethiopian slave girls, singing girls, and garments, so that the rate of the gold *dinar* fell by six *dirham*s. Having presented his gift he set off with the caravan. The sultan had committed him to the care of the emir Sayf al-Din Itmish, commander of the caravan, and he [and his companions] traveled as a self-contained company in the rear of the pilgrim caravan. When he had completed his Pilgrimage he remained behind for several days at Mecca after the ceremonies. Then he turned back but many of his followers and camels perished from cold so that only about a third of them arrived with him. Consequently he needed to borrow much money from the merchants. He bought several books on Maliki jurisprudence. The sultan presented him with horses and camels and he set off for his own country, having given away much wealth as alms in the two holy cities. Whenever his companions addressed him on any subject they bared their heads while speaking to him, according to a custom of theirs.

Al-Maqrizi, *Kitab al-Mawaʿiz*

The *madrasa* of Ibn Rashiq. This *madrasa* belongs to the Malikis and is situated in the Hammam al-Rish quarter in Old Cairo. When the [people of] Kanim (one of the communities of the Takrur) reached Cairo in the 640s/1240s proposing to make the Pilgrimage they paid to the *qadi* 'Alam al-Din Ibn Rashiq money with which he built it. He taught there and so it took its name from him. It acquired a great reputation in the land of the Takrur and in most years they used to send money to it.

Al-Maqrizi, *Kitab al-suluk*

[In 724/1324] Mansa Musa, king of Takrur, arrived proposing to make the Pilgrimage. He stayed for three days beneath the Pyramids as an official guest. He crossed to the Cairo bank on Thursday 26 Rajab [19 July 1324] and went up to the Citadel [to pay his respects to the sultan]. He declined to kiss the ground and was not forced to do so though he was not enabled to sit in the royal presence. The sultan commanded that he be equipped for the Pilgrimage. Then he came down. He paid out so much gold in buying what he desired in the way of slave girls, garments and other things that the rate of the dinar fell by six *dirhams* . . . .

On Tuesday 28 [Shawwal 724/18 October 1324] the caravan departed from Birkat al-Hajj for the Hijaz . . . .

On Friday 10 [Muharram 725/27 December 1324] the first pilgrims arrived [back from the Pilgrimage] . . . On Saturday the 25th the *mahmil* and the remainder of the pilgrims arrived with the emir Itmish al-Muhammadi, commander of the caravan . . . .

On 20 [Ramadan 744/5 February 1344] the pilgrims' *mahmil* set off from al-Birka. More than 10,000 Maghribi pilgrims had come and about 5,000 from the land of Takrur . . . .

On 15 [Shawwal 752/5 December 1351] the pilgrims' *mahmil* set off . . . A great company of people of the Maghrib had come, and also the Takrur, having many slaves with them, and among them was their king . . . .

117

During this month [Shawwal 819/November–December 1416] the caravan of the Takrur arrived to perform the Pilgrimage. They had with them 1,700 head of men and women slaves and a great deal of gold dust . . . .

In this year [835/1431–32] one of the kings of the Takrur arrived to perform the Pilgrimage. He travelled to al-Tur, there to embark for Mecca, but died at al-Tur and was buried in the mosque there. He was an upright man who recited the Koran frequently and had charity and kindness . . . .

During this month [Shawwal 842/March–April 1439] the caravan of the Takrur arrived with many slaves as well as gold dust. Most of them went to perform the Pilgrimage, having sold the slaves. Most of the slaves perished in the possession of those who bought them.

20. An Alternative Account of the Pilgrimage of *Mansa* Musa

IBN HAJAR AL-ʿASQALANI (1372-1448)

Ibn Hajar al ʿAsqalani (1372–1448) composed a biographical dictionary of important individuals who died in the eighth/fourteenth century. His entry for Mansa Musa son of Abu Bakr, king of the Takrur, tells the story of his visit to Cairo, based on the accounts of al-ʿUmari and al-Maqrizi.

Musa b. Abu Bakr Salim al-Takruri, king of the Takrur. He came for the Pilgrimage in Rajab 724/July 1324. He was brought into the presence of al-Nasir, but refused to kiss the ground, saying: "I shall prostrate myself before God alone!" The sultan excused him, admitted him into his intimacy, treated him with honor and gave him ample provisions for [the journey to and from] the Hijaz. There was much gold in the hands of the people [in Cairo which they got] from the people of Takrur, so that the rate of the dinar fell.

He traveled in a caravan of his own. His people held him in awe. No one could speak to him except with head uncovered. After the Pilgrimage he stayed three months in Mecca, and returned. A great number of his men died of cold.

He borrowed large sums of money from the merchants when he returned [to Cairo]. A group of those merchants accompanied him back to his country to collect their money. He was virtuous and pious, and brought many books. It is said that the total money that he had brought

Source: N. Levtzion and J.F.P. Hopkins, *Corpus of Early Arabic Sources for West African History* (Princeton: Markus Wiener Publishers, 2000 and 2006), pp. 357–58.

with him was 100 loads [of gold], and he spent it all on his way until he ran into debt.

When he returned he settled all his debts. He sent many gifts to a group of Egyptian dignitaries who accompanied him on the Pilgrimage until he arrived [back] at Cairo. His gift to the sultan was 5,000 *mithqal*s. He was very generous and brought to the [Egyptian] treasury a considerable amount of natural unprocessed gold. When he returned he sent many presents of the Hijaz to the sultan. He treated him and his friends gracefully and with kindness and generosity. He did not leave a single emir or official of the sultan without bestowing upon him a sum of gold.

Musa remained in his kingdom for 25 years, and then his son for four years, then his [the son's] uncle Sulayman reigned.

21. Arabian Bandits Destroy the West African Pilgrimage Caravan of 1455; no Caravan the Next Year

IBN TAGHRI BIRDI (1455-1470)

The historian Ibn Taghri Birdi (1409–70) was the son of a senior Mamluk emir. His chronicle Hawadith al-Duhur, *from which the text below is taken, was written in continuation of al-Maqrizi's* Suluk.

On Saturday 22 [Muharram 859/12 January 1455] the first caravan of pilgrims arrived, its commander being Khayribik the Inkwell Holder (*al-dawadar*) al-Ashrafi, one of the *khassakiyya*. On the morrow the commander of the *mahmil* arrived with the *mahmil*, after the pilgrims had suffered many tribulations this year from floods, deaths of camels and brigandry. This year countless beings were taken so that the caravan of the Takrur was taken in its totality and not a single man of the Takruris returned, though they had been extremely numerous. As for the Maghribis, they fought vigorously with the Arabs. They took from the Arabs and the Arabs took from them, contrary to the caravan of the Takruris, for it was all taken because they dispersed and were taken unawares, so that all were captured and some of them were killed. There is no strength but in God. This is something the like of which has not been heard in these days.

[860/1456] In this year none of the Maghribis or Takruris made the Pilgrimage because of the looting and imprisonment by bandits which happened last year, as has been mentioned.

Source: N. Levtzion and J.F.P. Hopkins, *Corpus of Early Arabic Sources for West African History* (Princeton: Markus Wiener Publishers, 2000 and 2006), pp. 360–61.

22. The Death of a West African King, Probably of Borno, Is Noted in Cairo by the Last Arab Chronicler

IBN IYAS (1474-1524)

Ibn Iyas (1448–1524) was the last of the chroniclers of the Mamluk period. He saw the fall of the sultanate to the Ottoman Turks in 1517. The king of Takrur who died in 1474 was probably the ruler of Borno; the other major kingdom in Takrur at that time was Songhay, whose ruler Sonni ʿAli died in 1492. With the following brief notice, the tradition of Arabic history-writing about West Africa approached its end.

In Dhuʾl-Hijja 878 [April–May 1474] the news came of the death of the king of Takrur, who was one of the greatest kings of Takrur.

Source: Ibn Iyas, *Badaʾiʿ al-zuhur* (Istanbul, 1936), vol. 3, p. 91.

Index